NAVIGATING LIFE WITH ATTENTION DEFICIT DISORDER

MICHAEL'S MOM

A ROAD WARRIOR WITHOUT A MAP

TERRY ELIZABETH NOLAN

TATE PUBLISHING & *Enterprises*

TATE PUBLISHING
& Enterprises

Michael's Mom: A Road Warrior Without a Map
Copyright © 2006 by Terry Elizabeth Nolan. All rights reserved.

This book is designed to provide accurate and authoritative information with regard to the subject matter covered. This information is given with the understanding that neither the author nor Tate Publishing, LLC is engaged in rendering legal, professional advice. Since the details of your situation are fact dependent, you should additionally seek the services of a competent professional.

Book design copyright © 2006 by Tate Publishing, LLC. All rights reserved.
Cover design by Rusty Eldred
Interior design by Chris Webb
Author photo by Karl Stambaugh

Published in the United States of America

ISBN: 1–5988636–8–1
06.10.20

PRAISE FOR...

"Parents of children with ADD should thank Terry for painting the portraits of our lives with the fine silk brush she has used. As we laugh and cry with her, too tired and stunned to pen this ourselves, we enjoy a therapeutic journey into our own parenting pitfalls and triumphs. Those of us blessed with our own spirited children share a little secret . . . we become outstanding parents—among the best you'll find. Terry shares her tips and techniques through the lens of her Road Warrior adventures.

"I place this tops on the list of required reading for anyone involved in nurturing the spirits of these misunderstood children. It is a much-needed break from the usual "dys-" and deficit. Instead, parents, aunts, uncles, grandparents and teachers may shift gears and celebrate the spirit and talent of our gifted explorers and pioneers. If you are embarking on your own journey, you'll gain from Terry's lessons learned. If you are well into your own adventures, you can cut back on the therapy bills and simply buy this book."

Chrissy Aull,
Founder, Wye River Upper School

"Terry brings hope, laughter and strength to the journey and offers a unique and engaging point of view brimming with love, wanderlust, and spirit."

Rev. Carol Callaghan, Deacon in the
Episcopal Church and Special Needs Educator

"Love saves the day. This time at the hands of a mother who refuses to let her son's ADHD Diagnosis become her family's death sentence. Armed only with an open heart, an atlas, and her two children, Terry Nolan sets out on a road trip that changes *fear and loathing* into love and understanding. Read this book and you will know more about ADD than most doctors. And you'll also learn a thing or two about the inner strength inside all of us that usually goes untested. This book is a profound inspiration on so many levels."

Danny Tepper
Creator, The FlashPhonics Learning System™

MICHAEL'S
MOM

To Michael

For opening my heart and mind and for giving me the courage to love more deeply than I ever imagined possible.
I celebrate your differences!

Acknowledgements

Thank you to everyone who has encouraged me throughout the ADD battle and the writing of this book.

For Duffy Weir, who read my first draft, offered invaluable advice, saved the day with the cover and believes the message of life with ADD is so important. She is a sister in this battle and a true friend.

For Cindy Stambaugh, my "editor in chief." I am forever in her debt! For endless hours, laughter, tears and editorial direction, she is my prayer partner and a dearest friend. I also thank her family, Karl, Lynnie and Lori for their sacrifice of her time and attention.

For Susan Wilford, with love and gratitude for welcoming me with such open and loving arms. LYLAS.

For the commitment of Judy Berrang, Michael's guidance counselor, trusted teachers Mary Catherine Cole, Colin Stebbins and Larry Cassidy and for the guidance of Dr. Bruce Shapiro, Dr. Roma Vasa and Dr. Robert Blatchley—I am grateful. You see Michael's enormous potential and cheer us all on. You're our "Dream Team."

To Mark and Linda, our blessed family and to Carmen and Xonia, two beautiful and spirited souls, thank you for respite from the road.

For Bob, Michael's mentor and friend, who has generously been an inspiration and encouragement to us all.

For Gerry Chiaruttini, Susie Dillon and Danny Tepper, your comments set me straight; I appreciate your valuable editorial eye and the time you devoted to the reading.

For my mother and father, who by example showed me the importance of commitment and gave me wings, and for loving Kevin, the children, and me with all your hearts, I thank you.

For Tracy, Suzy and Sandy, sisters and friends.

And Tracy and her family Bruce, Jeff and Lindsay for sharing life on the road with us and loving Michael and me always, and in all ways—exactly as we are! You're the best!

Ashley, Michael and Christine, I thank you for your patience and encouragement during the writing and driving process of this book. Forgive me for things that went undone and thank you for understanding my need to tell the story. I love to see the world through your eyes. I am grateful to be your Mother. I love you!

My soul mate and forever love, my anchor in any storm, Kevin, my husband and best friend. Like the giant sequoia tree, you are solid and well-rooted. Thank you for loving me unconditionally!

TABLE OF CONTENTS

FOREWORD

Attention Deficit Hyperactivity Disorder (ADHD) is a brain disorder that manifests in developmentally inappropriate levels of attention, activity, and impulsivity. It has been recognized since 1987. Its roots lie in hyperactivity (Minimal Brain Dysfunction) and inattention (Attention Deficit Disorder). The concept of ADHD continues to develop.

It is now recognized that this is a lifelong disorder. The behavioral manifestations change as the patient ages. Early manifestations center on activity and attention. Later manifestations are in the areas of socialization and organization. Criteria for the early diagnosis of ADHD in preschool children are still being defined.

Few children with ADHD have attentional problems only. Many children have additional problems with motor, emotional, and behavioral function, academics, and socialization. Consequently, each child has a unique disorder.

Each family of a child with ADHD undertakes their own journey. They face many challenges. This book represents one family's experiences. Some families face easier journeys, others face more difficult paths. Michael is doing well and his journey continues.

Dr. R. Bruce Shapiro
Kennedy Kreiger Institute,
Center for Learning Disorders,
Baltimore, MD.

PROLOGUE

More than 7% of United States schoolchildren are diagnosed with Attention Deficit Disorder (ADD), Learning Disabilities (LD) or Attention Deficit Hyperactivity Disorder (ADHD). That is over five million children who struggle with conventional learning! Over one-half of these children receive medications to accommodate these disorders, and along with that come the challenges of side effects.

Physicians, pharmaceutical companies, teachers, families and friends become acutely involved in the treatment and management of the child's disorders. Fortunately some people are educated about and understand the disorders but some do not, which again creates many more challenges for the children and their families.

Most parents are unprepared for the challenge of raising a child with any of these disorders, let alone a combination of them. Parents need hope in the wake of diagnosis, they need to know they are not alone and isolated by ADD/ADHD or LD. How do you teach and reach the child with ADD? How do you protect their fragile self-esteem? Behavior modification or medication? It's a unique decision, depending on the individual issues, but most often there is a delicate combination of the two. These are the questions all families with developmental issues must face.

Michael's Mom, a Road Warrior without a Map, is a first hand account of my experience with an ADHD/LD son for the past fifteen years. My youngest child has also been recently diagnosed with ADD so I now plot the course for two through the complex ADD/LD world.

This book is a journey into the unknown land of disorders through our mission to conquer all fifty states before Michael graduates from high school. Thinking and living outside the box is necessary for parental survival and the understanding and management of daily life with ADD.

Michael's Mom, a Road Warrior without a Map was written from deep within, seeking order yet finally surrendering to disorders. It was difficult, even painful to put this journey in writing. I feel vulnerable and exposed but also mercifully released from expectations—mine and societies—through the honest telling of our story.

It is my greatest hope that *Michael's Mom* provides encouragement for other families challenged by ADD and optimism in the face of isolation, exclusion and differences. You are not alone! I also believe the message of ADD so realistically portrayed within, vitally important for educators, friends of families struggling with ADD and the medical community. Perhaps by educating people outside daily life with ADD, I can create awareness and ultimately acceptance and inclusion—hope for all people, young and old, challenged by ADD. Or is it blessed by the gift of ADD!

1

LIFE, COME UNDONE

Life comes undone. Life perfectly planned anyway. Shifting like quicksand beneath my feet. I could pretend that all is well. All is normal. I'm good at that. Raised by a long line of great pretenders, normal is, after all, a relative term. Life, never as predictable as we hope it will be.

What am I thinking? Am I even thinking clearly at all? To pack up my Suburban, leave the Chesapeake Bay and travel west, across the United States not once but TWICE with my Attention Deficit Disordered (ADD) children in tow. A mother, alone. To prove what? To whom? Perhaps I need to prove something to myself.

So many unanswered questions! Will the miles and days on the road provide the answers? Is a mother's love alone, enough to pave a new road for her son? Have I lost myself in being a wife and mother? How do Kevin and I survive the challenges of ADD? At forty-five, I'm suffocating under the weight of life with special needs, un-charted and unexpected?

My spirit has grown dormant. I no longer know who I am other than "Michael's mom."

Since my ADD son was a little boy, babysitters, nursery school helpers and teachers would query, "Are you Michael's mom? May I have a word with you?" My chest would constrict, the feelings of fight or flight rising in me, knowing what was coming. Michael simply would not fit into their program; life lived according to someone else's standard, someone else's design, and high expectations. He chafed at their ways and their rules. He was different, gloriously different, but I didn't know it yet!

Michael's testing at a private elementary Prep School was a perfect example. The Director of Admissions was so prim and proper in her designer dress and highly polished shoes with her auburn and grey hair pinned high in a tight bun. She radiated good breeding and classic taste. She set up a simple combination of shapes and colors for Michael to follow. Then she mixed them up, expecting Michael to remember and repeat the pattern. Instead of following these deliberate directions, he challenged her to see if she could do it. Covering the blocks with his small hands and rearranging them to fool her. Needless to say, the Baltimore matron kindly informed us this was not the preschool program for our child; coloring within the lines was strongly encouraged there and our son clearly did not fit their form. Our strong-willed young son was making himself known loud and clear, very early on. He was impulsive, spontaneous and outspoken. Traditional, highly structured blue blazer venues would not be allowed to mold my son in the well-bred way society expects.

I have little recollection of relative ease raising Michael, the impulsiveness, anxiety, confusion, social anxiety, multiple sets of stitches, broken bones and angry moments, moments that rage like electricity. Frustration at every turn! Like a runaway train, ADD becomes life, full steam ahead, sometimes careening dangerously out of control. I was brought to my knees, knowing that in this fight for survival, Michael and I were broken and our spirits lost. I realized for the millionth time that he was rarely invited to a birthday party or second visits to a playmates home. Isolated and alone. It was so arduous sometimes . . . words I barely speak out loud. Heartbreak for us both. Our hearts and lives inexplicably entwined as only a mother can know.

Michael's medical files are cartons thick, documenting the details of his seemingly life long struggles. First, second and third opinions sought in our effort to save our ADD son and reignite his broken spirit. I'm a walking encyclopedia of Michael's mental and physical health histories. I know them by heart, just like I know my own, able to rattle off a myriad of medical and behavioral details for the last ten years in a single breath. A Superwoman of disorders! As I search for order in our disordered life.

Mother and son adrift . . . can we find our way back to each other? To once again share a common language . . . the language of love. Our interactions are often seeped in strife, unable to realize the simple joy in spending time together and revere the positive attributes of his ADD challenges. Michael's ADD "reputation" is hard to overcome and our tapes seem to play the same old show over and over again, reruns in the worst degree. To recognize, celebrate and appreciate our differences is what I seek from our Road Warrior travels. I know the road speaks, I have heard it before. I embrace the journey ahead, knowing the mission I'm on matters.

. . . .

In the Nineteenth Century, the ADD characteristics of excessive energy, out of the box thinking, creativity, risk taking, spontaneity and fearlessness were admired. The explorers, the inventors, the warriors, the founders were all likely ADD. Life in the nineteenth century was lived in the environment most ADD people flourish in—wide-open spaces and the great outdoors. The world and society were open and receptive to creativity and spontaneity.

In the twentieth century, all this changed for these pioneering ADD warriors. With industrialization came structure, routine and organized indoor classrooms. Learning was now done in a controlled and restrictive environment, with rote memorization and passive student role. Work, education and nutrition accomplished in an assembly line fashion. Industrialization was ADD's worst nightmare come true, ignoring creativity, independent thinking and natural curiosity! Hence, there was an explosion in the number of people diagnosed and medicated for ADD in the mid to late 1900's, now isolated by the classification and stigma of mental illness.

ADD is a neurological disorder and chemical imbalance, unable to be diagnosed by a single objective test, either blood test or marker on an MRI. Additionally, there are frequently co-existing disorders that accompany ADD including depression, anxiety, dyslexia, conduct, oppositional defiant disorder and finally bi-polar; making diagnosis and treatment more complex. Theories suggest there is a strong genetic component to ADD, since until the 1900's, ADD traits were the ideal characteristics to possess to live in the highly unpredictable and inventive culture of that time. Boys are also more commonly diagnosed with ADD than girls and frequently have the added hyperactivity component. ADD symptoms are present 24 hours a day, seven days a week, year around and it is currently the most commonly diagnosed behavioral disorder in children, affecting roughly 3% to 7% of school aged children, or well over two million kids. *Shire U. S. Inc. *ADHD and the Family: A Blueprint for Success* Florence, KY. 2002

ADD is not from bad parenting or lazy children. ADD children, and adults, are just wired differently, uniquely. And many of them exceedingly brilliant, even genius. Dr. Edward Hallowell, a foremost expert on ADHD tells these children "they have Ferrari brains with Chevy brakes!" Creative and brilliant thoughts processes, moving at exceedingly excessive speeds; generally un-harnessed from linear thinking. A significant number of adults today are learning of their own ADD, finally a diagnosis, and a name, for something they too have battled and couldn't understand. Unfortunately, damage was done to these adults, as children with undiagnosed ADD. Often called stupid, bad or lazy by teachers and peers, their self-esteem was under constant attack by society's expectations of fitting the obedient, bureaucratic mold. The jury is out for the twenty-first century ADD child. With the shift to a technology-based society underway, the inventors, pioneers and out of the box thinkers are once again esteemed. Video gaming and split second thought processing could rejuvenate the wounded ADD soul and restore pride and confidence in their impulsive and creative selves. As Danny Tepper taught me, "'Go ahead let society underestimate these kids and they will blow right by you, their 'Ferrari brains' on full throttle!'" Acknowledging that these ADD minds are the engines behind the significant cultural, societal and scientific changes their genius historically represents.

. . . .

My world seemed so small and my life so narrow as ADD consumed our family. Our daily routines revolved around ADD management. Color coding, prompts for remembering upcoming homework and tests, organizational skill building, social skills training and regular teacher meetings are all necessary components of ADD life. Between school, doctor's appointments, Children and Adults with Attention Deficit Disorder, CHADD support meetings and medication regulation, ADD and special needs is a full time job.

Ritalin, Adderall, and Concerta are the brand name drugs du-jour. Stimulant medications that seem to clear the fog in an ADD mind and focus their minds on the tasks at hand. These medications are thought to correct the chemical imbalance believed to trigger ADD and ADHD, allowing the area of the brain, controlling attention, impulses and behavioral regulation to function "normally." Medications are school mandated for many ADD children. Michael and I have vacillated in the great medication debate. On med's, off med's . . . with side effects and rebound, a common byproduct. Higher dosages, lower doses, no doses and changing times those medications are administered. Experimenting with antidepressants and anti-anxiety drugs, wired, anxious and agitated when the medications wore off. He goes up and down like a seesaw, a human guinea pig. Can we go on like this? I am a mother seeking a happy child, not an expert in neurological and pharmacological sciences. I cry to see his eyes glazed over and his spirit dormant by the sedation of these drugs. The light inside him dimmed to fit the social hierarchy of school and allowing me to avoid the disapproving glares of other mothers. Would he self-medicate with nicotine, street drugs or alcohol without the prescription medications? My greatest fear! But with straight A's at the public high school, and National Honor Society, the stimulants scream success. The answers do not come easily, and is success solely measured by the report card and conforming to the expectations of others?

Adrift, I lived in small town America with meandering brick sidewalks, neighbors who knew one another, colorful rose-covered fences and old stone churches, the exact ideal of America. Why did I flee when so many flocked here for respite? What was on the highway or in the vast open west that would speak to me? What did I need to hear, to feel, to learn? Could Michael and I change course, was there another road available where the challenges of ADD are not the most recognizable street sign?

The grass always seems greener on the other side of the fence. But is it? Women I met on the road shared such heartache, telling me a different story. A mother without money to provide food and shelter for her children, I met her in Tucson. A homeless woman asking a fellow homeless man, "Shorty, do you need an extra sweater for tonight" in Santa Monica and finally silently watching a woman in a car at a convenience store in Indiana with an ugly black eye and frightening man next to her. These were not greener pastures. The ADD Road . . . a scratch in my consummate life compared to those women I met, a blemish on the facade of high expectations.

So much to see and learn and feel on the road, I want it all! Life lived on life's terms. The only way to know the truths I seek is Road Warrior travel, finding myself is the first step. Michael, too, sees freedom ahead, in the excitement of the road, a release from the ordinary, a chance to be his spirited, spontaneous and curious self in the wide-open spaces of the Wild West. The answers for us both will surely come with the miles.

Michael, severely ADHD and Dysgraphic, the writing form of Dyslexia, has faced endless challenges adjusting to social situations, school environments and even family life. His positive characteristics, creativity, high energy, resourceful, trusting and sensitive with a good sense of humor, are so often overlooked, misunderstood, and lost in expectations—classic issues for the ADD Child.

A teacher in the third grade held his math paper up to the class saying, "Look, Michael makes his four's like a kindergartner." The class roared in laughter. At him. As if that would help him change his awkward learning style and improve his performance. Instead, he got off the school bus that same day with his shoulders slumped forward, beaten back again by society's rigid code of education and the lack of compassion and judgment by a trusted teacher. Michael, it turned out, was a whiz at mathematical calculations not writing skills, his Dysgraphia not yet diagnosed.

"Blah, blah, blah" is what school sounds like to him. A foreign language uttered by teachers for long increments of time, with Michael unable to leave his desk or speak a sound. Every impulse and nerve standing straight up crying out to move. To be somewhere, anywhere, but here! His ADD traits work best in a hands-on, active, learning environment. A living classroom of sorts, with movement, variety and physical applications to problem solving.

A next door neighbor invited all the neighborhood boys

to play in her front yard right next to our fence, but did not invite Michael to join in. He watched them play basketball with the saddest eyes a mother could ever see. I cried for him in the shadows of the house, excluded, because he is different, ADD. Impulsive and unpredictable, then isolated.

The strain on our family is enormous. We walk on eggshells, afraid at any moment our family will crack wide open, the fragile shell broken beyond repair. It has taken every ounce of love and energy to bring him this far. I am drained and emotionally exhausted, yet willing and able to fight the good fight for him . . . to my last breath. Michael tells me, "I used to dream a lot, now I don't dream so much any more." It is his redemption and maybe our family's that I seek on the road ahead.

Acceptance for Michael, and for me, for who we are and not by what I hoped we would be. Should have, could have, and might have, such a dangerous place to go amidst ADD. Letting Michael be Michael, and celebrate with joy, his uniqueness. Patina and not perfection. His self-esteem, buried in the rubble of his life, found and realized. Recognized to be the gift, I truly know he is inside. And to reclaim his dreams as his own even if they are not my dreams or society's dreams for him. Redemption. For Michael. For our family.

Ashley, Michael's older sister, a rising college freshman, my super achieving, beautiful, blonde and blue-eyed daughter with the brilliant smile who appears to excel at everything. Captain of the Varsity Tennis and Lacrosse teams and with high academic achievements, Ashley roars on with grace.

It all seems like it comes with complete ease to Michael's untrained eye. He believes he cannot compete with her. Yet, he also looks up to her, deep down wants to be like her: popular, talented, steady, and at ease with her life. Ashley has shown Michael endless patience and unconditional love. A trained Peer Mentor at her boarding high school, she learned all she could about helping teenagers with life's issues with her brother in mind. Knowing and understanding ADD is a road she too would be traveling, despite not being diagnosed with it.

Michael would taunt and engage Ashley in annoying ways, aggressive, shocking, anything to get her attention or her favor. He finally got her attention when the straw that finally broke them both came crashing down. Her endless patience exhausted, she physically took Michael down to the ground in a locked hold and told him to no longer mess with her, ever. His ADD would be no excuse! A small miracle, the wall that stood between them collapsed. Literally. He respects her, listens to her and reveres her strength.

Michael now makes regular calls to Ashley, his personal cheerleader, closest confidant and source of strength, late night phone support that encourages him when he has been beaten by life and cheering him on to another day.

Ashley, achieving, pushing, making up for the trauma caused by her brother by being excessively good, what does this stress do to her? She is seventeen, but feels the responsibility of a thirty year-old, an old soul in a young body. Her smile seems frozen like a beauty queen. She hides her own worries deep inside because Michael's issues monopolize us. The center stage lights always reflecting and set on Michael.

Ashley is excited for the rich, wide-open possibilities for her life. I mourn losing her to college, understanding that she will never truly be mine again. Or was she ever really mine at all?

· · · · · · · · · · · · · · · · · · · ·

Our Road Warriors' odyssey began like most great ideas— out of pure exasperation! Exasperation being a daily byproduct of family life amidst ADD. Me, forever trying to keep the peace and give our family hope in the face of this turmoil. I recommended to Michael, a goal to visit all fifty states before finishing high school. It seemed brilliant, and a perfect idea for an ADD, books-challenged kid to experience life hands-on; learning, feeling, seeing! A living classroom of life. Carpe Diem! We would do it, and do it together! Regional destinations, short side trips all began in earnest to check off the states on our fifty states log. Slowly but surely we made progress. Every family vacation even disguised by my motivation to conquer "new states."

Many months of planning were necessary for these long trips west: travel guides, the Internet, Googling sights and working around school schedules. Friends and family all enthusiastically shared advice and encouragement for our adventurous ideas. What to see, how many miles per day and reservations or no reservations? Life, on life's terms. My head was spinning with the obstacles and limitless opportunities of what were we undertaking.

Road Warrior Wisdom:

* You cannot plan for everything, so be flexible. Be spontaneous and open to the experiences you are trying to have. Keep your cell phone charged in case of an emergency.

I could plan the trip west to the nth degree with all the finest tools, a trendy palm pilot, high speed Internet on my laptop or a global positioning system (GPS). However helpful these technological tools seem, none can predict the path of the restless ADD child. Their behaviors and potentials are off the radar screen. Our course west would necessarily be charted by them.

Travel offers us the ability to see, experience and learn hands-on life's most important lessons. It is not the content of the sights or learning that is our aim on the road, but connection and application to ourselves and our lives that matters. Something we both need to discover. A mother alone with her kids crossing the United States, was I truly crazy? Every night, the news shows broadcast the latest tragedies, victims and injustices of random acts. Can we survive the unknowns, safely? Although safety in my life is a very relative term, I silently will away my fears and press on.

Westward Ho!

2

EXPECTATIONS

Expectations have filled my life, high expectations. The oldest of four daughters, I was held to the highest standard, under the greatest glare and a role model to my younger sisters. Expected to conform to the rigid standards of 1960's traditional parents. I was called to task for any attitude or behavior not fitting the norm of the well-bred young lady I was raised to appear to be.

Strong willed, like Michael, I chafed at this control, these unbending expectations. But, like a solid iron in a raging hot fire, I was bent and molded, succumbed to a will that was not my own. Allowing my spirited, wandering self to be buried under a delicate mask of a well-bred young lady, a frozen smile, so like Ashley's today, perfect posture, legs crossed at the ankles and timely thank you notes. Accouterments demanded of debutante society.

Matching everything for my three sisters and me, dresses, pinafores, pants and skirts in the same fabrics and colors times four! It was all the rage by fashionable 1960's moms. To be molded into the image of our mothers. Gone were choices, individuality and will. I was pressed and dressed to appear the same as society. My strong will was pressed and dressed by a force stronger than mine, a will, not my own. I could pretend with great believability that this is who I was meant to be, forever squelching the voice inside me. The voice that screamed to me, reminding me who I still was. The girl in the mirror, someone I no longer recognized; my reflection . . . a mask. Safely under lock and key for now were my wandering spirit and strong-will.

Unsteady as a teenager with my strong will securely under wraps, I embarked on a devastating relationship with an abusive boyfriend having lost the strength or self-esteem to fight back. I believed it was OK to relinquish control to someone else, to bend to their will, their whims, and their forever high expectations. My spirited soul yearned to break way, as I plunged into darkness.

Why wasn't I thinner? I already dieted to extremes. Prettier? I hopelessly followed the latest fashion and make-up trends. Perfection, my goal. There was always someone, something, more; I just could not keep up. Although I tried endlessly, still looking for the girl in the mirror to reflect who I was inside.

My parents and paternal grandparents became alarmed by my loss of self, but were unable to reach me and draw me from the abuser's grip. Why I would deserve this never really entered my consciousness. Maybe I did deserve this or just not know better, my spirited voice, silenced by now. Besides, I rationalized; he really does not mean those cruel things, attractive and smooth talking, the chameleon could be on his good days with my guard gleefully going down. Young and in love is what I thought I was at eighteen, precariously perched as the road crumbled beneath me. I was lost, and in search of the compass to my soul, yet there was no map out.

A sprained blackened arm later and a fragile mind, I found freedom from his grip. I ran with a tiny splinter of courage not tainted by others. I was not hopelessly lost after all. Somewhere inside I still screamed and I vowed to find the map back, to that voice buried so deeply.

Rebuilding lost hopes, dreams and trust was a painfully slow process. Step by step, mile by mile, I rebuilt myself. Like a toddler learning to walk, one wobbly step at a time, I slowly ventured out into the world of expectations again.

My investment advisory career began immediately after college and provided new direction, saving me from the previous abyss. My career began in a small town, which gave me strength and courage, and rekindled my will and ability to grow my own life. I learned to thrive independently.

Upon my college graduation, my parents wisely told me that after the expense of my college and with three more tuitions for my sisters, I was literally on my own. Their love, support and encouragement would be with me always and unconditionally. But financially, it was over. My financial umbilical cord was severed, never to be reconnected. This was one of the greatest gifts they gave me that day long ago. Despite being frightening for them to say and for me to hear, I once again reached inside myself, finding strength, courage and a will to press on. Forever forward, step by step, mile by mile.

As a poor college graduate with a new job in a new town, I moved into the Y.W.C.A. in downtown York, Pennsylvania. Excited by the prospect of dorm life again, I eagerly unpacked my new, used red Datsun B-210 of all my worldly possessions, one suitcase of "power suits"; it was the 80's after all and, my monogrammed briefcase and navy pumps, now long discarded. I had arrived. I was ready to face the jungles of Corporate America. My job at the local stock brokerage firm waited.

My concrete walled room and metal frame twin, with "No-Talking past 9:00 p.m." signs posted, seemed like a prison sentence. My mother helped me to settle in that June day, like that was perfectly normal, never showing pity for me or sharing the fear she felt for me. Was she doing the right thing simply leaving me here? Perhaps cutting the financial cord had been too harsh, too sudden? She hid her tears from me until later, when alone in the dark she would worry. Worry for her child, a mother's best friend.

My mother, her reflection I recognize as my own; where

my strong will comes from in the first place. A long maternal line of women desperately wanting to share their minds and energy on adventurous endeavors yet sheltered and contained by society's expectations. Not easily content with the status quo of womanhood.

Raised a Philadelphia debutante, my mother too, had dreams of the happily ever after story book ending. A strong-willed oldest daughter too, with bright red hair and an effervescence that overflowed. She was not your traditional well-bred young lady. She was raised by nannies and staff because her own parents were emotionally withdrawn. She screamed for her will to be heard, excelling at everything, hoping to win their applause and chafed at society's strict mandates for her, the limitations and expectations.

But with an alcoholic Irish father and wealthy, aloof, well-groomed Main Line mother, her happily every after was not to be. Turmoil and strife faced her at every turn, unpredictability and unknowns a daily way of life. There was no loving hand to guide this willful daughter. My mother, nineteen and in college, seized an opportunity for love and attention and wed my father.

Her will was again put under lock and key. Her dreams no longer her own and sadly not shared by her young husband. Four daughters and one miscarriage in five years, she conformed fast to life's expectations.

Very little money, isolation and a quest for survival, my mother's strong will re-emerged in the early 1970's. She raised her four daughters to be compassionate, fearless, strong, independent and wise; able to support ourselves rather than risk dysfunctional dependency in a world of unknowns. She also taught us not to fear the unknown, it would surely happen, and we best be ready.

My mother educated and encouraged me to dream big. During the Senate hearings on Watergate, she would point to the television; observing and asking where the women's voices were and why their representation seemed slight relative to the somber dark-suited men. She, who lived her teenaged life in the 1950's of few choices for women, fought with every fiber of her being to win choices for her daughters in the 1970's Equal Rights Amendment, a constitutional fight. She cried with despair in our kitchen when it was narrowly defeated.

My father was a hardworking man of the 1950's and shared a remarkable resemblance to Jerry Lewis. He was smart, bookish and privileged, with a wild side as well. He raced speed boats at a local Yacht Club, winning many races. His boat, the Cadet II, was named for his service at a military academy, where he was a confident young cadet. A small trophy cabinet and a highly polished silver sword are the only reminders of those glory days, when his youthful spirit ran free.

He too, had left his dreams behind, as one by one, new babies arrived—four girls by the age of twenty-six. Challenged to manage this brood on a bank teller's salary, his adventures in the years ahead would be diminished, mired in responsibility, and lost in a suburban abyss.

Paternal grandparents who lived around the corner in our bucolic small town were my saving grace. They so richly shared stories filled with exotic travel and wondrous adventures. I heard tales about the far reaches of the planet. I was always attentive, eager to dream and live vicariously through the great adventures they experienced. I realized an enormous world awaited me, right outside the town limits, creating in me a desire to dream and seek adventures of my own. Maps and roads could take me there, once I found the compass to my soul.

The reality of my parent's shared dreams were shattered when I arrived ten months after their wedding day. No longer husband and wife, or man and wife as they called it then, as though a woman was possessed by her husband. My parents realized the road to the life they knew was now and forever detoured by a colicky, strong-willed newborn. Their own teenaged selves were abruptly lost in my grating, needy wails.

As three more daughters arrived in the successive four years, the road back to each other seemed detoured, almost a foreign land. They were unable to read the language the map was in, an uncharted land filled with unknown.

A turning point for my sisters and me came unexpectedly. My parent's astonishingly seemed to have found a shared goal and united path, something foreign from my first fourteen years. My father, with a reignited sense of adventure, pressed forward, expectant and excited, as he and my mother planned two trips west. Would Westward Ho save our family? Would the miles, one at a time, speak the language they needed to hear? My parents certainly thought so, I hoped so. Hope being more powerful than anything! Westward Ho. . . . the cry as old as the hills.

Trips West One and Two for our family were in 1974 and 1975, two summers, thirty days each when the winds of adventure called this fragile family of six. We first crossed the United States the southern route and then returned home through the northern states of the country. The following summer, we crossed Middle America and returned through the provinces of Canada. Life lessons, lived on life's terms, for us to possess as our own as we grew into women. These would be points on a map we would need, as eventually we charted our own life courses.

It was not all glorious or wondrous in our rickety old Pontiac wagon with an equally rickety homemade blue wooden box strapped to the roof. Nearly driving off a mountain outside Reno, sisters bickering, with my mother in the middle seat refereeing and the wagon breaking down on the interstate delaying us for days and ruining our budget, our road warrior adventures were eventful. But, it was a shared journey, as a team, together. A family united with a common unbreakable bond, survival!

The glorious and wondrous moments I do remember came from simple things and random moments. My parents holding hands at Mount Rushmore, our morning milk being kept cold in a frigid alpine stream and simply laughing out loud as a family. Fleeting seconds of my childhood that still bring a smile at the sheer memory.

The road of the past taught me about simple things, love, laughter, togetherness and commitment. I learned that the roads we travel and the course we are on can be changed. What I hope the open road can say now. The road speaks clearest to me, can Michael and I press on, our direction clear and united on the ADD road we travel?

3

Surrendering to Disorder

After twelve months of plans, dreams, and what ifs . . . we are off! Our second Trip West. I am actually a bit nervous this morning; did I finally bite off more than I can chew? Am I really ready for the road ahead? Exactly what I am driving into, I just don't know. The unseen umbilical cord that tethers us to home is cut, sending us into the great unknown.

I am shedding my shriveled old self like a snake who sheds a tired worn skin. I have removed all my jewelry, except for my twenty-year anniversary band and a plastic no-name watch. I jettison my hot rollers and hair dryer knowing that is not the road I am taking this trip. My makeup is gone, along with my manicured hot pink fingernails. My pink and green *Lilly* life, cast off. The only nonnegotiable holdover is cliché blonde high-lighted hair that covers my "premature" grey, from shock or stress, I'm not sure, but I do know I earned it. I hope to hear with a new voice and see with a new heart what the road has to share with me.

My dented green Chevrolet Suburban with ninety four-thousand miles is gassed and ready to go. An atlas of the United States is the only map I need. At the eleventh hour, I break down and buy a Yakima roof carrier, presumably for more space in the car, but in reality it gives us permission to bring more stuff! Big mistake!

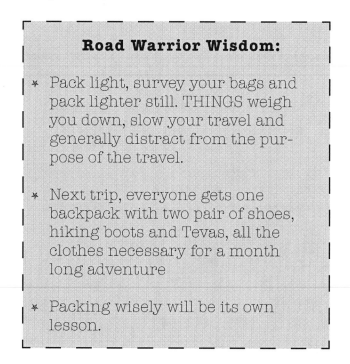

Road Warrior Wisdom:

* Pack light, survey your bags and pack lighter still. THINGS weigh you down, slow your travel and generally distract from the purpose of the travel.

* Next trip, everyone gets one backpack with two pair of shoes, hiking boots and Tevas, all the clothes necessary for a month long adventure

* Packing wisely will be its own lesson.

Kevin tucks us into the car with a bittersweet feeling, questions running through his head. Am I now acting as impulsively as my ADD children? Is this a midlife crisis amidst ADD? Why am I running? When am I coming home? Am I coming home? And his worst fear, unspoken, am I running from him?

. . . .

Meeting Kevin was for me, love at first sight. I feared the rush of feeling that free fall gave. Would I be lost again as in the previous relationship, under the weight of expectations? Do I disguise my feelings for him or abandon myself fully to the love he so freely gives? I am tentative and unsteady in his world of realistic expectations and unconditional love.

Kevin is sensitive, easy going and generous with salt and pepper hair and bright blue eyes. He is the kindest man, wearing his heart on his sleeve, unashamed to let his true self be known. Comfortable with himself and a knack for putting others at ease, he is friendly to every single soul he meets. From homeless to C.E.O. Kevin is an equal opportunity friend. There is no one I would rather be lost with.

Travel, wanderlust and shared dreams of wide-open spaces dominated our courtship. Packed on a whim for a romantic weekend "kidnapping" to some exotic locale or hiking Cadillac Mountain in Acadia National Park. The colors and wonders of the world magnified intensely in the glow of our love.

Kevin's first opportunity to meet my parents and sisters was on a chartered sailboat in Newport, Rhode Island. We would be sailing the Narragansett Bay to watch the America's Cup time trials, boating being a passion of my parent's. Westward Ho so long ago, rekindling shared goals for my parents. A forty-two-foot sailboat with ten people aboard for a weeks journey, equated to four point two feet of space per person! Either we would become engaged, or I would never see this handsome and adventurous young man again.

A trip to Maine in August without reservations was the final test of compatibility for us. We longed to climb Cadillac Mountain and sightsee around Mount Desert Island. In a four-seat, Toyota Supra sports car, we embarked on our journey of excitements and unknowns. Unable to find rooms in the booked solid high season, we resorted to sleeping in the Supra with the hatchback open. In sleeping bags under the star filled dark Maine sky, we dreamed together, shared dreams about what life together would be.

We were engaged one month later. Our wanderlust and adventurous spirits continued into newlywed life. Shared hopes and dreams, talks to all hours of the night and a deep, unwavering respect for each other's personal needs. Other than who made dinner after work each evening, newlywed life was bliss.

Happily Ever After, the story goes. The bedtime fairy tale that brainwashes an innocent young mind. I believed it with all my heart, feel adrift without its hope filled reassurance and mourn the unrealistic nature it created in me. Life comes undone, unraveled bit by bit and thread by thread by the reality of life with an ADD, Learning Disordered, (LD), and anxiety-riddled child. Kevin and I suddenly on a course unknown, a language misunderstood, un-charted terrain from my fairy tale dreams of happily ever after with the man I love.

At age eight, Michael was diagnosed with ADHD, Anxiety Disorder, Dysgraphia and Connected Language Disorder. Disorder was our past and now, assuredly, our future. Disordering life ahead for my family of five. My carefully constructed exterior image was about to crumble.

The emotional chaos of ADD/LD would have torn many couples apart, divorce being a common byproduct of parenting special need's children. A divorce lawyer informed me that she has not had a custody battle over a child with special needs. Parents torn apart tossed in the storms of ADD. We jealously guard each other, knowing the battle we are in is raging on all sides. We mourn the loss of tranquility but press on, united in the storm. We had once walked and talked and shared our great heart's desires. Our shared and individual dreams now set aside, our time and energy consumed by Michael's needs. Over dinner, over coffee, pillow talk and urgent calls, many conversations relate to the challenges our family faces with life amidst ADD. ADD has become our language, we speak it fluently. Yet, we stay anchored to each other in the storms of ADD/LD, knowing we are his warriors. Kevin and Michael look forward to their morning walks and midnight talks, a time to reflect and reconnect at the beginning and end of each day, a special time they share. As united warriors, we blaze this unexpected trail together, finding our way on this unknown road.

Westward Ho! The cry calls as old as the hills.

4

READY OR NOT

The first few miles of the journey are boring, reminding me of the chaotic and fragmented existence I am running from. So much is going through my mind as Michael, fifteen and Christine, eleven and I blaze our trail westbound. Kevin and Ashley will join us when we reach California. Ashley is seriously questioning the sanity of her mother and our endeavor.

The big picture is overwhelming, looking all the way to California on the United States map. So I break it down into single steps, mile by mile, one mile at a time, a life-skill that has saved me many times before. Just drive! I will see what the road brings.

Traffic in Annapolis and Washington, D.C. slows our progress, road construction and crazed East Coast drivers! I am going mad in the first 100 miles. I close my eyes and pray for patience when I want to scream bloody murder. Road rage already? But I realize it is rage inside me at the injustice of it all. Judgment. Isolation. Exclusion. Special needs. We are broken and wounded by society's expectations.

How will I make the 3,000 miles to California? I slow my pace, my mind and my expectations and the trip begins to flow. The rhythm of the road soon takes over. This is my second summer driving west across the United States. Last summer,

Michael and I went on a solitary journey, mother and son, to further his fifty states quest. I know I can make a difference and reach him to teach him, one-single mile at a time.

Our trip west was filled with talking about life, bonding in shared adventures, and creating lasting memories. Self-esteem, the buzzword of ADD life, now realized by learning new life skills, one mile at a time. For Michael, his focus and attention usually on failure will succeed in this fifty-state cross country quest. I will not let him fail. Failure being too prevalent too known in his ADD world. The seemingly ever-elusive success would be found in the miles and days ahead.

I started a Success Journal for Michael. A personal notebook to write the fleeting experiences of success. Success hard to come by, and rare for an ADD child to recognize in themselves, never enough moments of success to cling to and build upon. Michael has a reference book of his accomplishments, to remind him of his extraordinary potential. Creativity, sensitivity, a brilliant mind and genuine interest in helping people and animals; large parts of who he is, recasting the voice inside that tells him otherwise. A single, wobbly step, a mile at a time, one success at a time, we record his achievements.

Historic Route 66, with shabby, neon lit motels boasting of 100% refrigerated air and twenty-five cent Magic Fingers mattresses, the St. Louis Arch, Graceland and vast National Park treasures. Michael and I saw it all last summer. Kid-friendly and fun for us both, together we conquered the road as a team. Returning with Michael and my new language, souvenir rocks, shared funny moments and most of all, hope. Dawn was breaking through the dark moonless night offering me a glimpse of promise.

Learning what a unique adventure cross-country travel is, and remembering the amazing experiences gained from our first journey, I have included Christine this summer. This is a major undertaking since Michael and Christine absolutely do not get along; their personalities mix like oil and water. They look identical with their round freckled faces and dark brown hair, you know they are siblings. Yet, in the genetic lottery of life they absolutely believe this to be false.

Christine's mere existence, her simple breaths annoy Michael to no end, and she feels the same. They regularly taunt each other in a twisted dance, the music only heard by their ears. He wants to rule her, control her, and make her conform like society does to him. But Christine, my spirited child, like her long maternal chain attests, cannot and will not be tamed.

Christine, being the youngest, is most competitive with an intense desire to be first. Brilliant blue eyes and a round cherub face, born late in our child bearing days, she is a child of privilege, the financial struggles of early family years over. First Nolan to the top of Moro Rock! Only Nolan child to complete every hike! First, best, only it dominates her vocabulary. Her ambition consuming her like a drug, needing the rush it gives. A waiter in Hawaii told Christine to watch what the older siblings do and then do it better. He, also being the youngest of three, appeared an expert. She takes his message to heart as gospel.

Can these two children co-exist on the road for long miles ahead? Michael, awkward and prone to anxiety, seemingly unable to do anything right by society's standards; a loner by nature or by exclusion? Christine the Great, with no mountain insurmountable, no challenge forbidden, ready to conquer it all, confident and gregarious.

There is too much to see, to feel and to learn on the road to leave her behind. Our trip west makes this a perfect opportunity for Christine to see life, real life, lived on life's own terms.

Mountains and missions, deserts and cities, crazed drivers and mothers, Elvis and Owl. Raw. Life on life's terms. And so we travel on searching for hope and seeking redemption.

5

ADD Squared

Christine was also diagnosed this spring with ADD, without the hyperactivity component. The day-dreamy, social butterfly, girl variety, oh joy! The prospect of going down this lonely road with her now torments me. I know from experience the judgment society, friends and family have towards ADD/ LD children. Can Christine and I face this challenge and not be crushed by it? I desperately want to protect Christine's joy filled drama queen personality. Besides, what is wrong with being a dreamer? Isn't that what we all wish we could embrace?

I encouraged Christine after her diagnosis to keep the new ADD regimen of medication and diagnosis her personal business and not that of her classmates or the busy bodies of the world. Besides, Michael and I had been through the judgment gauntlet for years and I realized that well-meaning, as well as mean-spirited people, and even some family members, would surely take a side and voice their opinions, educated or not. Judging her, judging me; avoiding her, avoiding me; it's the same old song just a different tune. I am determined to protect her too.

Christine clearly does not agree with my advice and decides to take life on . . . on her own terms. In her middle school classroom that first morning after diagnosis, Christine immediately stood up and announced that "I am ADD, taking medicine to help with it and that's that." The drama queen performance of a lifetime, *Academy Award* winning. The sides would soon be drawn. Her friends, real or phony; my friends, real or phony; would make themselves known, all too soon.

The preppy little school Christine attends is picture perfect. A staunch and energetic Headmaster; and committed patient teachers make it a safe and productive learning environment for most learning styles. Opportunities abound for hands on learning in bright, friendly classrooms with small group instruction to encourage the children to thrive, each with their own unique ability, and each recognized for their singular special talents. However, there are certain parents I dread most when I hear this ADD news.

Mothers who grace the hallways with the sole effort of furthering their child, the social climb already underway with her as director. Expectations and goals of major achievement are set high in the independent school arena. Success is measured in very defined ways: socially, athletically, academically and even as a representation of the parents' own standing. As if these beautiful and innocent children are little ambassadors to their parents, status symbols to add to their collection of worthy pursuits and valuable things. Children now adrift, tangled in a web, unable to be themselves or make their own friends without great success or achievement to show for their very existence. A new generation for high expectations to curse. ADD does not play well in this world. It is viewed like a communicable disease, catchy and contaminating—someone or something to be avoided.

Not invited to birthday parties, or play dates or to share best friend secrets. Time would tell indeed, the reality of middle school girl world harsh enough already, the weight of a gossipy glare heavy or social exclusion defeating. How do I keep Christine from the crush to come? Does it have to come at all? Or can I fill her up with enough love to save her, too? The ADD road map I was handed so long ago, crumpled with age and stained with tears is reopened to now plot Christine's course.

Children have an innate need for justice and truth, easily spotting lies a mile away. Children with ADD know they are different without even knowing precisely why. This is revealed to them repeatedly by teachers, peers and parents with our own high expectations. They also compare themselves to peers and siblings wondering why they themselves cannot seem to get it right when it appears to come so easy to others. When we finally sat Michael down to explain his ADD/LD diagnosis, too many years too late, Michael said, "Oh, I thought it was an accident at my birth." He knew instinctively, he was wired differently. I am disappointed with myself for not revealing or explaining his diagnosis sooner. Had this been childhood cancer, I certainly would have revealed all probabilities, knowing society's empathy for physical illness versus the stigma and isolation of mental illness or disorders. As Michael's mom, I hoped I could make everything all better if he or I just tried harder, even believing I could fix this, fix him. Yet, unintentionally, I made things worse by not empowering him earlier with an informed diagnosis. It devastates me to think of lonely moments Michael endured thinking he was an accident at birth.

Upon Christine's diagnosis, she was told the news immediately after her physician phoned, her reply, "Ok, I guess that's why math is so hard." And off she went to play, not discouraged. Yet. She struggles regularly with mathematics, so I put her in charge of our finances for the trip. Christine is responsible for keeping a log of our daily expenditures. Gasoline, food (two meals a day), lodging, tolls and souvenirs, right down to the penny we track every expense. She aptly records each item and sorts the receipts asking to sign the blank charge card slips (it does start young). I hear regular gasps from her calculations, unable to comprehend the amount of money we are spending on this road warrior adventure. I hear the numbers and think what a bargain this therapy is.

Psychologists. Fat ones, thin ones, males and females, young and old. Even Blinky, nicknamed by Michael because he blinked excessively. Psychobabble talks, with Michael again just hearing "blah, blah, blah." None of these well-intentioned Ph D's able to speak Michael's language, to reach him. It was not until we were at the final straw with therapy that a small miracle happened. Dr. B.

Dr. B is a boy's man! He is a gentle giant with a grey balding head and a handshake like a vice. Dr. B. loves hunting, fishing, Labrador Retrievers and Alaska, activities ADD warriors like Michael appreciate. At the first appointment, Michael and Dr. B hit it off instantly when they both shared the same favorite place in these vast United States—Jackson, Wyoming—Michael's dream locale. Someone who spoke the same language . . . Outdoors. Spontaneous. Spirited.

I do not know what they talk about every week, but I do know Michael would not miss that hour for anything. Small miracles, single steps, one mile at a time!

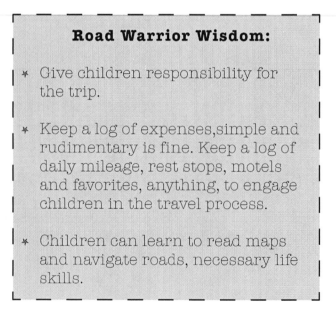

Road Warrior Wisdom:

* Give children responsibility for the trip.

* Keep a log of expenses, simple and rudimentary is fine. Keep a log of daily mileage, rest stops, motels and favorites, anything, to engage children in the travel process.

* Children can learn to read maps and navigate roads, necessary life skills.

6

Unplugged

Michael and Christine have picked places in the car separated by a full row of seating, each guarding their coveted little domains. Michael cannot keep his hands to himself, so he selects a bench seat with extra space to fiddle and move.

Each child has brought along "fun bags," self-packed bags of amusement for the long car travel ahead. I learn a lot about each child by what I see in their fun bags. Michael has a single overstuffed canvas bag with a Maxim magazine, a top 100 swimsuit model catalog, summer reading books and X-box inspired comic books. A boy/man is in my back seat. Reading for Michael being a colorful and interesting pursuit, less words and more pictures telling the stories he wants to hear. Christine has brought three small fun bags, stressing the seams with zippers wide open, pushing the limits, chafing at rules. Her fun consists of a beloved childhood doll, summer reading books, the dreaded school required math workbook, colorful drawing pencils and paper, a DVD player and movies in case the life in prison penalty is lifted, and finally, small nick-knacks for make believe. The storybook fantasy of happily ever after is still alive in her world.

Snacks and a cooler filled with ice cold water bottles are at the ready. My disputed rule of no DVD player solidly enforced.

We are unplugging from the pace of life as we know it and redirecting our senses to new experiences. Life lived on life's terms. I explain that the real world is outside their window and to fully appreciate it, they need to slow down, eliminate electronic distractions and sharpen their senses. They too look at me as though I am mad, questioning my stability. Maybe I am, we certainly shall see.

On we travel, Westward Ho.

Welcome to Virginia, not a "new state" for our checklist. I am not ADD, others may say Obsessive Compulsive Disordered, (OCD) so setting goals and reaching goals are my specialty! I am not daunted in the least by fifty states. I am mother to two ADD children! I fully intend to complete the task at hand. We will reach all fifty states; I absolutely will not let us fail.

We skip the Virginia battlefields because life's already a battlefield of its own. We surely do not need to be reminded of that. An American History textbook of Michael's made the trip with us. The book has barely been opened the spine unbroken, a testament to the fact that books are jumbled words, unlikely to teach him anything new but add to his already easily frustrated learning challenges. I marked various pages of historic events that will compliment our travel. However the only one who truly appreciates this gesture however is me! Although Christine, very capably reads to me anything I ask, she insists she is only practicing for future Hollywood stardom. The Civil War and Virginia's place in it, presidents born in Virginia and segregation, we are on a roll.

Michael suggests that we start keeping a list of "dumb named towns" we pass. Sounds like a plan, and at least something that encourages him to be attentive and keep an eye out the window as life goes by. Christine reads from a book of the fifty states to share information about each "new state," what we call a state that qualifies as a check on the fifty state logs. After all, what is the point of visiting a new state and not knowing what to appreciate? Learning without even realizing it! I sneak the lessons in like strong medicine hidden in decadent chocolate ice cream.

```
┌──────────────────────────────────────┐
│         Road Warrior Wisdom:           │
│                                        │
│  *  Stop at welcome centers upon       │
│     arrival in a state.They are friendly│
│     centers with clean restrooms,      │
│     fresh hot coffee and water, plenty │
│     of state information and compli-   │
│     mentary maps and brochures.        │
│     Plus, locals are more than happy   │
│     to share their own state favorites.│
└──────────────────────────────────────┘
```

State signs pass, "Welcome to North Carolina." A pit stop, at Steak and Shake for our afternoon meal which suspiciously the children think will be lunch and dinner combined. They are right; eat up, miles to go before we rest for the night. Kevin's only hard and fast rule is "off the road by 9:00 p.m." and I honor that request for the safety of us all.

Eight in the evening on day one, we check into a no-name motel on the border of Georgia. There are steel rails on the sliding door for "safety" and we are overlooking a local Hooters restaurant. Michael smiles and fogs up the glass pane, hoping to spot departing waitresses from our window. We are not staying in fancy hotels on purpose, this is not a trip of privilege, but a trip of life, real life, to be lived and experienced on life's own terms.

No-name, even neon lit chain motels teach us life on life's terms. Gunshots outside our motel last summer in Saint Louis was our only close call and even then, I tried to reassure Michael and myself that surely it was just a car backfiring! A kennel club checking in right after us in Sergeants Bluff, with barking 'til the wee hours, planes landing overhead at LAX or the railroad track right behind our motel in Flagstaff that I swear made our little room shake every time a train passed. Life, on life's terms is not always the easiest road. But who ever said the road of life was easy or what we expect in the first place.

Tomorrow, Atlanta, and a morning visit to Kevin's Aunt Carmen. Michael's minimum mileage for a day is 400 miles, our mileage today 606, giving us a fudge factor of 206 miles. I crawl into the shoddy, worn bed with the ugly orange comforter and drift instantly to sleep, dreaming of opportunities in this wide open world.

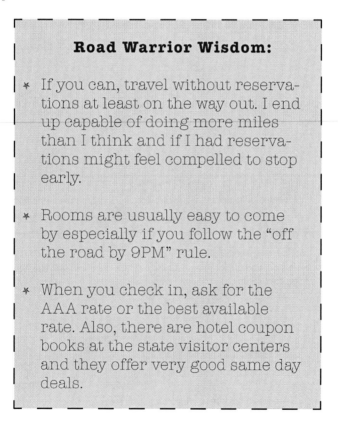

Road Warrior Wisdom:

* If you can, travel without reservations at least on the way out. I end up capable of doing more miles than I think and if I had reservations might feel compelled to stop early.

* Rooms are usually easy to come by especially if you follow the "off the road by 9PM" rule.

* When you check in, ask for the AAA rate or the best available rate. Also, there are hotel coupon books at the state visitor centers and they offer very good same day deals.

Michael's Mom

7

RHYTHM OF THE ROAD

Day two, the break of dawn, I'm wide awake, packed and ready to go, happy to say "so long" to the dreary little motel and hit the open road! The children look at me through bleary eyes unable to comprehend the need for such an early start, after all this is vacation. What state are we in again? A big southern breakfast of biscuits and gravy wakens them and we return to Interstate 85 south. The rhythm and pace feels good . . . I have found my groove again behind the wheel.

I have an altered mind set when traveling long distances. The more miles I drive seem to release in me a "runners high." Endorphins. Driving gives me a sense of control as I live feeling daily life careening out of control. Control over something, anything rather than surrender to the chaos of it all. After the first two hundred miles or so, travel becomes effortless, easy, even relaxing. Undaunted by the miles, I sense I have a clear direction, am making progress and finding the answers I know the road can give.

"Welcome to Georgia," peach signs abound. We visit Kevin's Aunt Carmen and what a joy that turns out to be. She is a talented watercolorist and sculptor and a beautiful soul. Carmen is in her late sixties with an admirable youthfulness and free spirit. Her silver hair, colorful dress, warmth and radiant kindness greet us. Michael ambles through her cozy Southern home, from room to room, seeing and touching her sculptures and playing with her grandchildren's toys freely left out as a welcome mat to any child who enters her world. She is relaxed and patient with Michael, her generous spirit comforting.

Christine Marie is named for Carmen's mother, Marie, an "almost" Catholic nun and this is an important moment for Christine. Their strong family heritage and shared artistic talent link them together giving Christine wisdom for her future. Christine sees who she is, where she comes from and what she can accomplish, in that glorious time of life when everything seems clear and possible. She feels her heart beating with potential. Her future, bright and alive, the dreamer recognized and valued. I am mesmerized by their conversation. A benediction of sorts, as Carmen blesses us and our journey ahead.

We visit the City of Atlanta and Olympic Park. The Olympic Rings are on the ground and part of a fountain, so much for the planned photo-op. No volunteers for the CNN tour, instead Michael and Christine unanimously opt for the World of Coca Cola tour and enjoy the old fashioned fountain soda's best, refreshing in the humid summer sun. Our final stop in Atlanta is "The Underground," a trendy retail shopping zone developed by my friend Duffy.

. . . .

Friends, true friends are a precious gift. Especially when you have a child or children with ADD or LD. I count these true friends on a single hand. Many "friends," even family members from our previous life, life before ADD, before outbursts and unpredictability, have fallen away from us. No longer friends with our family, fearful that ADD is contagious, some even harboring a seemingly bitter pleasure at what they perceive to be our weakness. Life with ADD is not easy, in fact it has brought Michael and me to our knees, but there we found strength and courage we might not otherwise have learned. The pain of invitations to birthday parties and special events addressed to everyone in the family except Michael. Seated alone at the lunch table, or avoiding the lunch room altogether, too brutal a social jungle to navigate on your own. Cruelties that make the ADD kid or any kid but especially Michael feel more isolated. Perhaps they are uneducated about ADD, perhaps they are satisfied with their superficial status quo or perhaps they do not want the responsibility of a relationship that requires giving more than you receive. He cries out to be accepted, to be "normal," whatever normal is.

A horrible part of me daydreams and even envies what normal would have looked like. My tall preppy son, the captain/president of something with a pretty brunette girlfriend and tons of friends. Not the normal I signed up for. I am on a detour, a foreign land to the fantasy land of happily ever after. I never had a map for this journey, I am traveling on an unknown road… lost. Maybe, my expectations were not normal in the first place, what is normal after all? Life with ADD is normal for us.

True friends come in like angels, usually sharing some common thread of an ADD or LD child. Friends that accept personal imperfection with sensitivity and compassion and are undaunted by different. Incomparable kindness, patience, forgiveness and unconditional love radiate from these lifesaving friends. When my ADD child spray paints his name on the side of my girlfriend's house and she still hugs him with might. Inclusion for Michael with invitations to family events, outings and childhood birthday parties. Laughter, and not condemnation when Michael's Fourth of July fireworks display goes awry, hits the roof of a friend's house and catches it on fire! Michael is my big rambunctious puppy who just wants to be loved, to be accepted, imperfection and all. Few, but true friends, these are powerful allies in the battle to save the ADD child and their self esteem. They share love, acceptance, inclusion and compassion mixed with joy and laughter.

Michael sorely dislikes cities where his ADD and hyper-sensitivity escalate from the frenetic pace of life, causing him to feel claustrophobic. He is intensely unsettled by the home-less population, pushing their life's possessions in grocery carts and searching trash cans for food. He is angry and frustrated by society's lack of support and tolerance for them, a positive direction for his anger and frustration. Michael compassionately served homeless men and women of the Washington, D.C. area in cooperation with a youth church mission. These were not just the homeless to him, these were people with names and faces and stories with hard roads traveled, he not only cared for them he respected them. Likewise, they recognized and appreciated his deep sensitivity and sincere concern for their welfare. Michael's sensitivity will be a gift when he is grown but it's a tremendous burden at fifteen, an old soul in a young body. He feels deeply the pain of others and carries it as his own.

On the other hand, Christine is completely fed by the ener-getic pace of city life, clearing her mind and focusing her atten-tion. Inactivity, boredom, and quiet spaces are too slow for her, prone to cause her attention to drift. Her senses are acute in the hum of the urban landscape, completely engaged in everything the city offers, and wanting more.

The very different faces of ADD.

We are leaving the city behind, heading for the calm of Ala-bama, southwest on the car's compass. A favorite road warrior moment, singing "Sweet Home Alabama" while driving through the state, it is blaring and we are rocking! Michael and Christine amuse themselves in the car, sharing the contents of their fun bags, playing cards and checkers on a makeshift carton table, actually getting along, realizing they are all they have in this unknown land, accepting and tolerant of each other's differ-ences. Change, a work in progress!

We enjoy a rest stop at the Bates Turkey Farm to learn how turkeys are raised, then an early dinner at the Bates House of Turkey. We order turkey dinner with all the trimmings, of course. Life and death on the open road.

Mississippi welcomes us. The state every school child loves to spell, M-I-S-S-I-S-S-I-P-P-I. The heart of Dixie welcomes us with soft southern accents that are friendly and warm. Ancient Magnolia trees in full bloom are bursting with fragrant white flowers.

More reading on civil rights, cotton gins and segregation, is anyone listening or am I talking to myself? Check, we have seen Mississippi. We briefly took the scenic Gulf route and wondered where the scenery was amidst the oil refining companies and glitzy casinos. On we drive, pure adrenalin flowing. Unknown adventures keep Michael and Christine on the edge of their seats in anticipation.

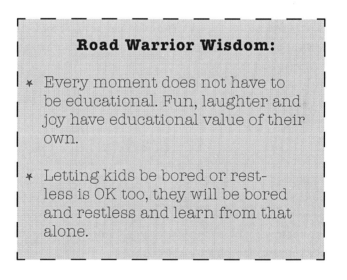

Road Warrior Wisdom:

* Every moment does not have to be educational. Fun, laughter and joy have educational value of their own.

* Letting kids be bored or restless is OK too, they will be bored and restless and learn from that alone.

Welcome to Louisiana, and still day two! We notice the French influence everywhere, parishes for counties and French script on signs and we suddenly feel we are on a European adventure. We are driving Interstate 10 to New Orleans thinking this will be our overnight stop.

We arrive in New Orleans, "The Big Easy" at 7:30, and the

pulse of the city is alive. The city is humming with jazz music, trumpets and saxophones groaning through the narrow cobbled streets. It is surrounded by water on three sides and actually settled six feet below sea level! Bourbon Street is packed and the smells of local Cajun cooking make my mouth water. We are disappointed by the wild and excess partying going on. In the street! Mardi Gras beads and masks adorn visiting tourists who appear to have had too many jell-o shooters and loose teens are chased on the open street by local police for crimes unknown to us. Michael is uncomfortable spending the night here so we take a family vote and the vote is unanimous, three to zero to drive on, not feeling safe here alone. Beignets and Café du Monde coffee with chicory at Old Jackson Square provide the power to go on and we are off once again. I call Kevin, telling him I look forward to returning to enjoy the gourmet cuisine, breezy jazz clubs and rare antique stores the city is famous for. New Orleans appears perfect for a romantic getaway.

Amidst the ADD/LD storms, it is vital that Kevin and I cherish each other and carve out special time together. Time alone, away from disorders to stay connected, with shared dreams rekindled. Our children recognize date night is sacrosanct; Kevin and I were here first and will be here when they are grown and gone. I wish I could admit we don't speak the language of ADD these nights but ADD is such a powerful influence it's impossible. But we have learned to catch ourselves when we've detoured to speaking fluent ADD. And return to the language of love. A strong marriage and a united front are essential for the strength to navigate and survive this ADD/LD road.

. . . .

The road leaving New Orleans is dark and forbidding over haunted black bayous. I question our decision to push on and hear anxiety creeping into the voices of Michael and Christine. Our first stop, there is no room at the inn, pushing us further into the dark, frightening void. Michael heroically carries on random conversation to comfort Christine. He is sensitive and gentle, seated next to her holding her hand, and trustingly she rests her head on his shoulder, no longer afraid, her big brother protecting her.

Highway signs read twenty-five miles to the next exit and it's already 9:30, a broken curfew, but only for our safety. I feel lost and alone in an obscure, alien land. We push on for over an hour, eventually securing respite near Baton Rouge. Finally, tucked and locked in; with every fiber of my body completely exhausted, crying out for sleep. Yet, our spirits remain intact, despite our exhaustion, remembering "the journey is the destination."

I am comforted hearing Kevin's voice on the home answering machine. So much for the joys of peace and quiet of bachelorhood he anticipated relishing. He plots our course each night on a United States map proud to boast to anyone who will listen what we are doing. He is not discouraged when he gets strange glances about our unusual adventure. He knows I am not mad, or at least hopes so anyway.

8

Laughter, the Best Medicine!

I awaken more tired than the past two days combined, my adrenalin buzz finally wearing off. Stronger, black coffee, now mainlined please, inspiration in a cup! The Waffle House is a twenty-four-hour chain and the breakfast café of road warriors. Whimsically, the restaurant's letters are spelled as square waffles. Gayle, our waitress looks exhausted. She is tall and gaunt with dark circles the size of craters under her puffy brown eyes yet despite this she still offers us a smile and a friendly southern welcome. I learn she works two jobs to make ends meet since tips for breakfast do not stretch very far. She is supporting two children as a single mother, her husband long gone with another woman. I must stop complaining about my own road. I sound petty and spoiled thinking I have it tough. Perspective now being everything as Gayle provides a reality check for me; her life appears punishing, with no luxury to flee to.

Michael and Christine are ravenous after the marathon of miles yesterday. They eat their fill of an "all star" breakfast including a southern favorite, grits. I leave Gayle an unexpected tip, hoping to make a difference in her day and to honor my mother who shares her name.

We share a brief photo opportunity on the banks of the Mississippi River as we cross to the West! We are officially west of the Mississippi River and share celebratory cheers all around. Michael can smell the West and is beaming. He knows the potential the West holds, it calls to him like road warrior life calls to me.

The bayous of Louisiana are interesting in the light of day. We cross a twenty-four mile bridge over verdant bayous, one of the longest bridges in the world. The bayous conceal their secrets in the dense, lush and primitive marshes. Alligators silently peer through slivered breaks in the water, stealthily seeking prey. Air boats course through the moss covered bayou with ancient Creole men fishing for dinner or maybe for their very existence.

Two near accidents—the first being my error as I nearly crashed into a stalled vehicle on the Mississippi River Bridge. The driver frantically waving me away as I swerve to miss him, a panicked look crosses his worried dark face. I'm distracted by the celebration of the river. A shocking thought crosses my mind: maybe, Michael and I are not as different as I thought.

My childhood report cards give hidden clues to our similarities. "Does not apply herself," "Needs her energy channeled," "Will not stay seated for circle time" signs that my own strong will and no tolerance for boredom in the classroom are not that different from my son's. Michael and I are usually like magnets, when facing different directions our energies push each other away, our interactions intense, believing we are opposites, and not like the other. Our past exchanges somehow seep back in and cloud over our latest attempts at meaningful ones. Can our magnets be turned over, to pull us together, unite us in a common goal? To see we are not that different, that we travel the same road.

The second near-accident occurs two hours later. We are spared a rear-end impact by a large red pick-up truck with oversized tires as the driver swerves into the dusty, dry median at full speed to avoid our car, slowed by highway construction. A giant dust cloud roars toward us, set on consuming everything in its wake, as screeching brakes wail. I gasp and take a deep breath to calm myself with Michael now on full alert; he, our self appointed guardian. I am instantly reminded to slow our pace. This is not *The Amazing Race* from reality TV. I ask myself silently if I am running from something or to something, and the question haunts me.

We stop at a Louisiana alligator house for a leg stretch and a reprieve from the road, particularly after our near fatal collisions. Michael bravely holds the baby alligator while Christine shyly pets it, keeping a safe distance. Two additional huge grown alligators lumber around, with Michael sensing they're on the lookout for prey, their beady eyes scanning the scene. Christine is thrilled to see an ancient, 114-year-old gator turtle, turtles being her favorite animal and camp mascot! The gator turtle is shaped like a turtle but with an alligator's coarse skin, webbed feet and angular head. While there, we meet three Louisiana State Troopers; one is a marijuana plant hunter by helicopter over the bayous. Michael and Christine marvel at the fact that they will not hold the baby gator, as they appear big and strong and fearful of nothing!

Road Warrior Wisdom:

* Hands-on activities create a real learning environment. Children, unaware of how much information they truly retain, not realizing they are learning something new.

"Howdy y'all," a road sign beckons. Texas, here we come. Everything does seem bigger in Texas! Looking at the map through southern Texas suddenly overwhelms me. How will I travel all those desolate miles as the sole driver? A brief panicky feeling hits me. What am I doing on these roads alone? Is this fifty states pilgrimage really working? Finally, one mile at a time, slowly and surely, I will myself forward.

The road less traveled seems the most frightening, with more unknowns and no maps to guide me, only instinct and heart to lead me. That is life with an ADD/LD child. I press on, like a blind woman struggling to see where I am headed, other senses on full alert, but without a clear vision. Driving like crazy, not fully knowing or understanding the destination of my heart, unable to chart my progress. Perhaps, not knowing the way gives me freedom, opportunity and vision to think and see outside the box. And there, we may find each other, in a place we'd least expect.

We find stray kittens at the Texas Welcome Center and Michael and Christine feed them leftovers from the car. Christine begs to keep one, pleading "we cannot leave them to die in this heat." I suggest she inform the welcome center of the kitten's presence and the kindhearted, elderly woman at the front desk assures her they will be cared for. Missy, our calico at home is the only stray we get to keep. Besides, I absolutely cannot have another breathing soul in this car! That will come soon enough, in California where our road warrior clan grows.

Entertainment on long distance road travel comes from a variety of elements, one being billboards. You follow them, look for them, miss them when there are none and are amused by whatever is being hawked on them. After watching billboard signs with a cartoon beaver for 172 miles, teasing road weary travelers about what to expect at Bucees Souvenirs I surrender to the stop. Water, coffee and everything Texas is offered at Bucees, all at exorbitant prices. As Christine notes, "Bucky chewed right through our wallets and likes bucks." Postcards home, to friends and family are mailed and coffee for me, make it a double, refreshed from our rest stop, we drive on.

Finally San Antonio and we are checked in at 4:30, a tremendous luxury to be off the highway so early. The children enjoy reckless pool fun, a desperately needed break from the road. We meet my mother's college roommate, Xonia, pronounced with a "Z," for dinner. She is a native of San Antonio, and is pleased to show us around, kind and generous with her time, and a heart of gold. Xonia has a deep Texas drawl that is warm and friendly and wears a loud, oversized Mexican dress. She's never married, yet completely relaxed with the children. They, too sense a kindred soul. Someone judged as different, spirited and confident in her own way of doing things. Her life lived on her terms, alone, but not lonely.

We enjoy a delicious Mexican dinner on the river and I, a very salty lime margarita. We embark on the riverboat cruise along the scenic Riverwalk to see the Spanish and Mexican influences felt everywhere. San Antonio is named for Saint Anthony, the patron saint of children and things lost. Southwestern shops, ethnic restaurants, flowing cypress trees and historic hotels dot the narrow canals, reminding me of Venice Italy, with twinkling lights crisscrossing in a playful way. Spanish moss weeping from the ancient trees adds to its haunting appeal.

The San Antonio Spurs are playing in the finals, so every television has the game on, the pulse of the city erupting with excitement. We have upgraded to a hotel since we are visiting Xonia, not wanting to embarrass my mother with coupon motel accommodations. Pretending once again to be the well-bred lady I was raised to appear. Returning to the hotel, I walk over a powerful air vent and my pleated Mexican skirt goes flying up, ala Marilyn Monroe. Michael and Christine think this is hilarious. My own facade falling away with the miles, I laugh out loud, at myself! Laughing together, the most wonderful sound in the world!

When did I stop laughing out loud, laughing at myself? Does the seriousness of everyday life with ADD cause me to miss the absolute joy of it? Life lived without spontaneity? My life and conversational ability seems to solely revolve around disorder-centered problems. Like an avalanche, ADD has swept me along, consumed my spirit and taken me down. I forgot the glorious sound of laughter, the renewal it brings and how good it feels to simply laugh and play.

I have an old wooden sign at home, "live well, laugh often, love much." It has been hung in the same spot for so long, I forgot the importance of the message. Not to take life so seriously that I miss the joy and spontaneity of it. The message I lost in the frenetic pace of daily life with ADD. Perhaps, extra doses of humor will take the edge off us all, funny, side-splitting laughter to cleanse our souls and eliminate expectations of perfection. Laughter is truly the best medicine. Tomorrow, "Remember the Alamo," today's lessons, priceless!

Road Warrior Wisdom:

* For long mileage days, have ample rest stop/sightseeing events in the middle of the day. It makes travel special and provides adequate time away from driving. We drive four hours or so in the morning, have a sightseeing event for three or four hours and return to driving until we are tired or it is 9:00 p.m.!

Michael's Mom

9

METAMORPHOSIS

Good morning San Antonio! We sleep in this morning, an untold luxury, with no crack of dawn departure necessary. I have lost track of what day today is; the days of the week are woven together like a fine tapestry of miles and states.

First sightseeing tour, The Alamo, and viewing the IMAX movie, *The Alamo, the Cost of Freedom,* provides us with a greater understanding and better appreciation of the memorial. For thirteen days, brave men stood against the massive Mexican army to defend Texas' independence only to end in brutal massacre. The cry, "Remember the Alamo" propelled Texas to action, and ultimately Sam Houston and Company secured its independence. It's a strong reminder to us that freedom and liberty are never free.

My sister, Tracy calls while we are visiting The Alamo, asking "Where in the world are you?" When I tell her San Antonio, I hear the excitement from her family in the background, cheering us on. They understand the ADD road is complex and unknown yet know we are making progress, and conquering it, one single mile at a time. They are supportive and proud of us, our closest compatriots on these western adventures. They will join us, for the third leg of this journey, beginning in San Francisco.

Tracy, with dark black hair and opaque freckled skin, you cannot immediately tell we're sisters, but in our robin's egg blue eyes, you know we are. We are fiercely loyal to one another growing up only fifteen months apart. Tracy, the recovered teenaged wild child, strong willed as well, turned "Aunt Molly," our family nickname for the quiet kind soul she is, her greatest concern always for others. Tracy is a geriatric Registered Nurse with the compassion of a saint and the patience of Job. She is organized, thoughtful and the peacekeeper between sisters. I could never have traveled this ADD road without her, a true confidant, giving the strength only a sister can provide. Tracy shares the tears I shed and cries her own, for Michael and me. Always reassuring me of hope ahead, she is a godsend. Tracy and her family share our love of the west and wide-open spaces. Hiking trails, climbing mountains and wanting to see it all without hesitation or reservation, our families kindred.

. . . .

I regress, or some might call it growth, shopping at the glass walled mall in downtown San Antonio. Christine begs me to browse in Forever 21. She is persistent, a positive ADD characteristic and will not let up on me, so into the store we go . . . Christine leading the charge, not taking no for an answer.

The trendy store has clothing that is foreign to my eyes. The tee shirts are paper thin and sheer, with sequins no less. When did lingerie become wearable outside the bedroom? I am lost in a time warp of matching dresses, conservative styles and a pink and green wardrobe. Nothing appears remotely possible for me to wear. Christine, my budding artistic fashion designer selects matching white peasant skirts and together we find the dressing room to try them on. I morph into a lighter person wearing the loose fitting, wandering skirt. Like a butterfly coming out of her cocoon. I twirl around as she insists we buy the skirts, letting go of old rigid habits with my ADD child's help!

Michael, in another part of the mall, is insisting he needs to buy a Zippo lighter "for security," he pleads. Somehow I cannot see fending off trouble with a Zippo. No Zippo lighter today as I remind him of our adventure with fire-starting once before.

In our undaunted quest to successfully complete Michael's fifty states goal, Ashley joined Michael and me, visiting New England states last year. Accomplishing two goals at once, as we checked states off Michael's fifty states log and toured college campuses Ashley selected. Her college choices were predominantly urban so only a few tours appealed to Michael. He absolutely will not attend an urban college, that is, if traditional college fits him at all.

In an effort to direct his immense creative energy, I encouraged Michael to begin an invention journal. A rudimentary doodling of inventions he would tell me he was thinking up; creative and wild ideas he believes could change society. Any and all ideas can be included; telling him there is no such thing as a stupid idea. How Michael learns best is by doing something hands-on, taking something apart and putting it back together. My engineer, of sorts! Seeing with different eyes what's not working in real life. I wonder to myself, what college would best suit him? Many colleges today are offering alternative learning environments and for that I am truly grateful. It is a new reality that educators are aware of learning styles and "differences" and embracing these students, encouraging their out of the box thought processes, while society still labels them with the stigma of learning "disabilities." College hovers close by, however, just keeping his dreams alive are goal enough for now.

Ashley and I completed a scheduled university tour and returned to Michael, who insisted he be allowed to wait in the car, swearing he did not have an ounce of energy left for one more walking tour. Armed with an I-pod mini and colorful comic books, I relented, trusting him to "be good." Whether boredom or just plain mischievous curiosity reigned, Michael started small bits of paper on fire in the car, with the never used cigarette lighter. When Ashley and I returned we smelled smoke but could not find the evidence. He shrugged his shoulders saying "It was really no big deal." I, his mother, his warden, was overreacting as usual. Boys will be boys or something like that; must I make such a big deal about a little fun?

With this memory in mind, I decide we will take our chances without the Zippo on the road ahead. Instead, Michael and Christine each select a new book to enjoy on the long dusty road ahead. Michael continues with a spy series he is interested in; doesn't every boy dream of being a spy! As Christine selects a book that also happens to be a summer movie she's seen and has pictures to prove it. They add their books to the fun bags, armed and ready, for the many miles to go.

Westward Ho, the cry continues. Despite, pleas to "stay one more day" we are off through God's glorious open west. The hills and rocks glow with life. This is the wild, Wild West, where untamed natural beauty abounds. There's a sign advertising "Horse Stalls for the Night, Inquire at the Best Western Desk," rest for all weary souls. The radio blares country music on two available stations, one in Spanish as we chase the setting western sun passing through one-horse towns dotting the West. The lyrics of Tim Mc Graw fill the car, "loved deeper, spoke sweeter . . . live like you were dying." Amen to that!

We gain one hour driving into Mountain Time. I love that, one extra hour, sixty minutes, three thousand six hundred seconds of something! It feels like a precious gift. We settle in a motel in Carlsbad, New Mexico, excited for our morning caving adventure. Local evening temperature is 103 degrees in the shade.

A fight breaks out between Michael and Christine over the remote control for the television. Any sense of sibling harmony seems lost. Channel surfing has gone hopelessly awry with reality TV bearing no resemblance to the reality of my life. Unnecessary electronic tension, I turn the TV off and we go to sleep.

Road Warrior Wisdom:

* Service stations in the west can be miles apart so you need to be prepared for anything. Always top off your tank when going into unknown long stretches, Death Valley for example where no gasoline is sold or Yosemite where the first station out of the Park had a price per gallon a gouging $3.95 for regular gasoline when the average price we were paying was $1.97 per gallon.

10

UNDERGROUND

Only our fourth day on the road and yet it feels like a journey already! Searching for woolen sweaters in the desert heat, we prepare ourselves for a tour of Carlsbad Caverns National Park, the largest cave system in the western hemisphere and a geologic masterpiece. I'm definitely way out of my comfort zone going one mile underground and traversing over two miles of trails but I persevere, not wanting Michael and Christine to sense my fear and trepidation about this great adventure.

Entering the Original Entrance of the cave, we descend underground down a spiral gravel path into the deep, dark unknown. There's a flurry of noisy birds screaming in and out of the small opening, seeking freedom and just as quickly flying back into the security of the cave. I have the same feeling in reverse, entering the cave and as quickly wanting to flee, back to the security the light and known world appears to offer. The rhythm underground ebbs and flows, like life. It is surreal here, medieval, dark and confining. Water created intricate handiwork as spires rise from the floor and fall from the ceiling. Silence shrouds me in a peaceful blanket with droplets of water offering a soothing refrain. We're lost in the shapes and colors of the tangled foreign landscape.

Michael leads the way through the blackness with a small

flashlight from his backpack. Christine hovers close to me, needing the security a mother brings. As we trek to the bowels of the cave, our spirits and senses are reawakened. I watch a spider weave its intricate web, delicate and fragile in the harsh damp air, wrestling with life's challenges, yet forging on, the will to survive so strong. Learning, we are capable of more than we imagine! We relish the experience of a snack in the cave café, our first (and last?) meal one mile below the surface of the earth. In the dark cave I find I am still brave, strong and courageous, a part of me I believed was lost. Strong enough I silently pray . . . for our long road ahead.

We continue on through Guadalupe Mountain National Park, an angry and forbidding landscape so hostile to life. Amidst the sun baked desert there is life-giving water feeding the harsh yet fragile ecosystems. The air feels like a furnace thus our brief hike is shortened. The formidable terrain is in sharp contrast to the cool, damp caves dwelling below. Life, struggling to survive extremes is something I know well.

We pass El Paso, Texas, scene of our stolen credit card shopping spree last winter. The phone ringing at dinner time, as the caller queried, "Is Mr. Nolan in El Paso using his visa at K-mart?" No! Ten thousand dollars of charges made in a short afternoon. Michael is asking for the hundredth time "did they catch the guys?" Black and white, he craves justice being cash register honest himself.

We see Mexico from Highway 10 and several roadway exits point to the Border. We clear two United States Border checkpoints searching for illegal aliens or suspicious people. "Do brothers count?" Christine wonders aloud. Looking inside our car, a mother with two ADD children, 2,500 miles from home and the chaos of travel apparent, I am a bit surprised we are not detained as suspicious!

In the footsteps of Billy the Kid, Kit Carson and other Wild West legends, we stop at La Postada in Mesilla, New Mexico, a stagecoach stop on the Butterfield Trail in the 1800's, and now home to fine Mexican grub. Ravenous, we eat our fill—after all this is lunch and dinner combined! Michael is intrigued with cages of colorful exotic parrots near our table, who "talk." Like Dr. Doolittle, he engages the birds, talking to them with spontaneous curiosity. I cannot overhear the words he's "teaching" them and can only wonder. Nearby, there's an aquarium of surly piranhas, with a "do not touch" sign. I watch his body ache to defy the warning.

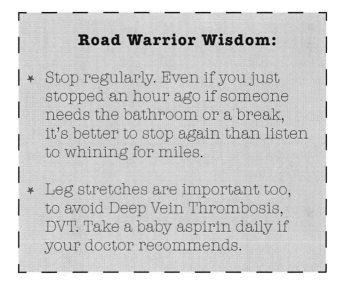

Road Warrior Wisdom:

* Stop regularly. Even if you just stopped an hour ago if someone needs the bathroom or a break, it's better to stop again than listen to whining for miles.

* Leg stretches are important too, to avoid Deep Vein Thrombosis, DVT. Take a baby aspirin daily if your doctor recommends.

Passing the Rio Grande River, there are more billboards, now hawking "The Thing," 170 miles. "The Thing" taunts and teases for miles, what could it be? Michael begs to exit at "The Thing," he has to solve the mystery, 170 miles of curiosity and seventy-five cents later he passes through the well-guarded gate to solve the mystery. He returns, proudly announcing his find… a mummy, a kitten and old cars, a junkyard of sorts! He will surely remember this roadside tourist trap, cheap entertainment along lonely Interstate 10 West.

We are listening to Delilah's call in radio show to pass the time, and Michael's amused by the lovelorn callers. Delilah is speaking to a forlorn caller about love gone awry. The young girl tells Delilah she is desperate to get her boyfriend back, completely lost without him. Delilah tells her to get a mirror; she'll wait, as silence reigns on the airway until the girl returns. Delilah tells her to look in the mirror and repeat after her, "I am somebody." Over and over like a mantra. Michael meanwhile has the visor mirror down, repeating and believing her mantra. "I am somebody," he exclaims with gusto! I watch in awe, as his self-esteem gets a necessary boost from the serene voice on the radio and long miles on the road. My son is coming back to me!

Christine has my cell phone desperately trying to call Delilah to make a dedication. I feel flattered, thinking it's me and our trip west she is dedicating a song to. She confesses instead, "it's Daddy who is so worthy of a radio love song dedication," missing him more than she shared. Deflated, I accept a serving of humble pie and on we go.

Tucson, Arizona is our stop, completing the day with 502 miles and by nine on the nose. The motel we check in resembles a neighborhood with entire families on the edge of poverty living together in the tiny worn rooms. The wallpaper is peeling, and a microwave oven on a miniature refrigerator next to the bathroom, encompasses the "kitchen." Two flimsy double beds with thin mattresses and threadbare tired bedspreads and a small TV on the dresser make up the rest. Bicycles are parked outside the locked screen sliders with the "safety" bar; and appear to be the parent's only source of transportation. Most of them are immigrants, illegal aliens and migrant farm workers chasing the American Dream. English is the second language in this "community" in Tucson. It is frightening for us to witness these families and realize the tenuous nature of life. We pray for them and count our own blessings, as we lock our door and drift to sleep. We plan to make California tomorrow. I am ready to see the Pacific Ocean after these hot desert days.

11

WE DID IT!

It is an amazing drive through the khaki colored Sonora desert filled with enormous Saguaro cacti, through Yuma, Arizona into the California wilderness covered in white sand dunes, all while hugging the Mexican Border. A paltry two foot fence marks the miles' long border and again, we pass through three Border checkpoints, without incident. Michael now seems eager to leave his sister here; her constant chattering is getting on his nerves, drained from the miles and days on the road.

The final trip into San Diego is a breathtaking climb over towering mountains descending into the Pacific Ocean. Giant boulders dot the landscape of this very windy road. We drive immediately to the waters' edge, running our toes through the warm silky sand and celebrate! We actually did it, arriving in San Diego in five days! I cry, seeing the immense Pacific Ocean and clap my calloused driving hands so hard they sting. I'm in heaven. We embrace a few Kodak moments and with perfect timing Kevin and Ashley call with congratulations.

Sea gulls sail through the soothing, healing, salty air. A Grady White fishing boat like ours streaks through the ocean, carefree fun on a Sunday afternoon. I am suddenly homesick for Kevin. Our dreams, I realize are not lost, just buried like golden treasures waiting to be found. Dreams born of true love, when we first walked and talked and shared our heart's desires. Our desires are created individually and as a couple, and we are anchored together able to weather any storm.

Michael looks relieved to see the California coastline. We made it safely across the United States and without the Zippo necessary to ward off danger! He still wishes we had left Christine behind, nudging her aside from our photographs. He believes this fifty-state quest to be his thing, this, a celebration of his success. "Oh well," he sighs as he steps aside to make room for Christine in his celebratory photo, his arm slung over her shoulder, silently bragging "I did it."

Christine beams proudly at her accomplishment, making it across the United States with her Mother and her brother, intact! Christine, who announced one week before departure that she does not like car rides, feels car sick after a two-hour drive to her Dede and Poppop's, and cannot possibly make it to the West Coast in a car. She did it; I can see her pride shine. She's matured two years in these five days on the road.

Michael is ready to check into a motel, eager to get out of the car, my homebody at heart. On the other hand, Christine, a beach girl, is ready to find a surf shop, energetically on to the next adventure she goes. We compromise instead with pool time, to cool off, a necessary release after hours cooped up driving. Michael and Christine are playing Marco Polo together as friends; it's a wonderful and glorious sight, learning together that we're all we have and doing the best we can, and that absolutely being enough. Returning to our room, Christine announces, "I have a pretty shadow," as Michael shrugs his shoulder. "Sisters!" Life, a work in progress!

Our memories for leg one are priceless with vivid reflections from our intrepid journey. I am proud of Michael and Christine, they've been amazing troopers. So many daily unknowns yet we've rolled with life, and lived on life's terms. Travel being the best education, ADD or not! Together we could confront and accomplish anything. Working as a team, with maps, navigation, finances, check in-check-out and decision making . . . a job well done! Points on a compass essential as their own adult paths will eventually take shape. My road warriors are my heroes.

Michael is my most seasoned road warrior and right hand man, who thinks any mileage less than 400 miles a day is a waste. He is always alert, brave, safety conscious and protective. Quite the honorable Road Warrior, I will travel anywhere with him! Forever a gentleman, he embraced and encouraged his little sister. Christine, who left the baby of the family and grew to a self-assured competent traveler in part due to Michael's encouragement. I have enjoyed the slow pace of their company rather than the hurried chaos we live at home. ADD now a precious gift, enjoying daily doses of witnessing and living life through fresh, innocent and curious eyes. Childlike wonder, lost to me since adulthood, this wonder- a feast for my soul. A kaleidoscope of small miracles I might miss with tired, jaded eyes, giving new meaning to the journey is the destination! "Are we there yet?" no longer mattering.

I wonder what will be remembered from this trip west, a family journey or their Mother's personal odyssey under a fifty state guise. A time of expectations crashing down under the weight of ADD . . . surrendering to disorder. Emotional chaos. Judgment. Bitterness at injustices no one seems to understand, the trauma and isolation an ADD/LD family feels. Yet, learning this bitterness is only poisoning the vessel it's in, needing to be released and seen only in the rear view mirror. Knowing with ADD we cannot live our life looking in the rear view mirror. Forward, forever forward must be our mantra! This journey, my personal odyssey to make sense of the life I live. The life we share as a family. To know what I am doing matters, is real and makes a difference. The battles I fight for my ADD children showing progress. Letting go of the happily ever after mirage, culturally ingrained images and crumbled myths, allowing the crack in my armor to show. To know being vulnerable is OK.

. . . .

"Mean girls" are not just a middle school phenomenon. Mean girls exist in our 30's, 40's and 50's, awaiting the opportunity to pounce if other social climbing shoes are not up to par or the perfect facade is cracked revealing difference. The latest, greatest, and most expensive designer fashions camouflage these spoiled middle-aged mean girls; something their teenaged counterparts only aspire to. High fashion and new found wealth equates power; power these Queen Bees cannot wait to exploit. A pecking order among peers is created, the perceived Queen leading the way, glancing at themselves passing any mirror, impressed by the reflection they see. Dropping subtle crumbs of influence, their poisonous sight scanning the horizon seeking to control or even ruin others who appear "different." I flee their staring glares, incessant cowardly gossip and harsh judgment. Perhaps they too have lost their way, under the spell of happily ever after, unable to find their way through reality and disappointment to truth, and are struggling to control their morsel of perfection left. Afraid, that if people see their true selves their own facade will crack wide open, revealing deep down, that we are all imperfect and unable to control as much as we think.

Patina! A scratch in a veneer that brings growth, character and enhances value. Antiques are full of patina and the more patina the higher its value. The joy of patina is embracing imperfections through an attitude of tolerance and acceptance for different and developing character with disappointments, imperfections and scratches to show for it.

I'm living on caffeine, which is coursing through me to keep pace, wanting to see and do it all. Why my haste? Am I on borrowed time? A midlife crisis of some sort? A daughter leaving for college? ADD, perhaps a precious gift and not the curse I thought?

12

LOST AND FOUND

San Diego is a fabulous city, and the Zoo turns out to be a must see for Michael, given his love of animals. We're thrilled by the abundant species of animals and lush verdant gardens. A bumper crop of newborns abound, attesting that life goes on. Christine, the first to enter the park upon opening, her competitive nature rages on as she jumps in front of Michael to stake the claim. He again shrugs, and shakes his head in annoyance. Sisters!

Michael's favorites are the orangutan. Their human-like appearance and behaviors fascinate him. Having studied them in school last year, he is thrilled with the opportunity to see them up close and personal. This is how Michael learns best, seeing, touching, feeling, and observing life hands on. I like the beautiful white swans best. They remind me of two mute swans I saw this past Valentine's Day swimming together in our creek. I was amazed to see this sight and asked Kevin if he put them there, as a gift to celebrate the day. He confessed that he wished he had thought up such a romantic gesture but he could not take credit for the stunning white swans, a glorious gift nonetheless. Swans, which mate for life, stay together through sickness, and weather all raging storms. Like Kevin and me.

We're intrigued by a funny little monkey swinging and

twirling on trees, falling on an older monkey to get him to play along. The older, bigger monkey pushes the tyke away not at all interested in playful, childish antics. I see myself in these motions and am ashamed. Frivolous moments seem so rare at home. My energetic and expectant ADD children so engaged in life's pleasures, and me absorbed in disorders unable to let go and play. Be impulsive; playful and spontaneous, everything good about ADD! I make another mental note to play freely now and when I return to captivity, sucked back into a world of decorators and designer shoes, the drum of high expectations, although now not my own. No longer dependent on the happily ever after, now cherishing life's possibilities simply in the day to day journey.

Michael relates well to animals and thinks being a veterinarian would be a great profession. He insists I call his guidance counselor at school right now to tell her, not wasting a second! He's not lost . . . just taking a different road! People are judgmental and complicated to figure out but not animals. Animals don't seem to judge him as harshly society does; they are not intentionally unkind or full of unrealistic expectations of him. He is compassionate and caring, and isn't love what conquers all? Could this be our answer, a hope for his future? I glimpse his dreams returning, with possibilities he envisions, in a future that suddenly seems real. He is happy and content here, a Michael I rarely see in the confines of home.

We must push on to Los Angeles where Kevin arrives in two days. I'll miss beautiful San Diego and hope to return for a longer stay. The familiar interstate calls once again, the California traffic congestion and people's fear of driving there is legendary. I am pleasantly surprised to find the highways a well-organized system of travel, even during rush hour. Drivers are more polite than expected and high occupancy vehicle lanes are simple to use for longer drives. The most congested and frustrating area was within the Los Angeles city limit. That takes hours and patience!

We stop for the night in Hollywood, a place of star struck dreams and profound disappointments. We want to walk Hollywood Boulevard but the significant homeless population wards us off. They are predominately teenaged boys and girls, with haunted, vacant eyes in grimy denim jeans and stringy matted hair, barely hanging on to reality. They look refugee thin from the drugs they are lost in, slumped under neon lit movie posters, hopeless and alone. Have they chased the elusive dream of the happily ever after in Hollywood stardom and lost themselves along the way? I want to ask where their mothers are. How did they lose their way and have no option but the street? Michael's anxiety is on full alert, his eyes wide and intent on the scene, feeling compassion and empathy, their needs appear so great. We pray for the lost souls outside our window, adrift and lost in a world of high expectations. And once again count our blessings.

No rest for the weary! We awaken early, ready to brave Hollywood in daylight. Arriving at Hollywood and Highland at 8:00 am, it's deserted, perfect for us. We see everything, without massive crowds or eccentrics dressed as their favorite Hollywood character parading around for tips. The children love the "stars" and Grumman Chinese Theater. They seem surprised Hollywood's so small relative to its legendary status. Christine selects her future star, a blank star on the sidewalk just waiting for her name. Christine is not dismayed about her Hollywood stardom dreams. Her drama queen personality is at the ready, honed by miles of emphatically reading aloud the boring history textbooks brought along.

HOLLYWOOD, the sign with forty-five foot tall letters staked in the Santa Monica Mountains has beckoned stars since 1923, and is recognized around the world. A guidebook promises a secret vista so we attempt to see the famous sign up close via the narrow winding reservoir road but the street is closed due to severe mudslides, some houses can even be seen perilously suspended on the crumbling hillside. Mudslides, Santa Ana winds, fires and earthquakes all present a challenge to the area environment. Signs abound on city buildings proclaiming its earthquake steadiness and warn of older buildings instability.

A tour of Universal Studios Hollywood, for a lighthearted day of spontaneous fun and laughter! A lesson learned from the little monkey in San Diego, fun, laughter and play having value all their own. We take the studio tour, basically the same behind the scenes movie tour I enjoyed thirty years ago on my family's vacation west, Trip West One, in 1974. It's a serious flashback seeing this through an adult lens with my own children in tow. We ride the tram tour twice, Michael not wanting to miss a single thing, fascinated by the inner workings of a movie studio. His passion and enthusiasm are contagious, he's now seeing stars…Hollywood dreaming, alive and well.

I call my parents from Universal Studios thanking them for their shining example of overcoming life's hardships, for perseverance, fortitude and commitment, to each other and to me. Grateful that they taught me a great love for this country and the tremendous opportunities that exist through travel and how to be strong and fearless in the face of unknowns. I learned patience, the power of commitment and how to read a map. These lessons I draw on now, practical and useful, for life, no matter what road. Travel, our best teacher!

We are anxiously awaiting Kevin's arrival in Los Angeles tomorrow, and then we will start leg two of the journey. Practically living out of the suburban the past week, a little housekeeping is in order before we head to the airport. Reminiscing our way through the debris lets us relive a few precious moments with laughter and reflect on the first week that flew by as we crossed the United States, from coast to coast, the long way! We have seen, learned and grown so much, discovering who we are and what we are capable of accomplishing, together and as individuals.

I have missed Kevin's smile, sense of humor, kind words and his touch. I am homesick for my husband! As the long days and miles pass, I appreciate how blessed I am to be married to him and what a wonderful life and family we've created together. It's not perfect, certainly not as glamorous as it sometimes appears to others, a Ken and Barbie world, but nonetheless strong and intact! We remain united together, "sharing a brain," as Ashley confesses, facing anything that comes our way. Diseases, disorders, mean people, judgments, it no longer matters- we will face it together and continue to grow stronger, like swans swimming together in the stormy seas called life.

Kevin respects my wanderlust and encourages my personal growth, knowing the stronger I become the stronger our family is. I realize that to travel 3,000 miles seems insane. But, it's what I needed, to be on the road, to hear my voice that has been dormant under the strain and chaos of our daily life with ADD. A language lived, yet not spoken, forever unyielding to the high expectations of the outside world. The futile attempt I make for Michael and me to be someone other than who we are meant to be. The many miles "alone" are an accomplishment I am proud of, not because it is special or singular, but because I heard my voice, the voice that once dared to dream, to live, to march to the beat of a different drum. My reflection, someone I again recognize. Lessons learned and earned on the open road.

Moments, not things will be my mantra now, my prayers, uttered, never ceasing, like a nun with her rosary, over and over again. Mothers are forever thinking and hoping they can fix everything and make everything better: skinned knees, bee stings, best friend trauma or ADD. I cannot make everything sea glass smooth. I found emancipation from self and society imposed high expectations, for me and my children. By releasing my own excessive expectations, we will surely beat them all. A moment of complete freedom comes with this realization and I'm elated and liberated. Mothers are the keepers and guardians of a family's hope.

13

REUNITED

We are thrilled to greet Kevin at the airport. Michael, like a puppy with his nose pressed firmly to the window, his eager and open face anticipating the embrace and affection of his father, missing the bond of their morning walks and midnight talks, time shared with his "head coach." While Christine, our artist, holds a handmade "Daddy" sign, like the limousine drivers do. Welcoming him with kisses and missed you, everyone talks at the same time, so much catching up to do. Kevin enters our travel seamlessly. In fact, it seems he's been with us all along, in spirit.

Does Kevin see the change in me, the miles of soul searching wrought? Externally, it's obvious! I am wearing my Forever 21 outfit from San Antonio with hippie chic chandelier earrings purchased in Hollywood. My highlighted hair is breezy and flyaway, no longer couture and rigid. The mold broken wide open and the mask removed! Does he see inside me, I wonder? See what the miles and days have taught me? I am changed . . . surely Kevin sees this.

We tour ultra-chic Beverly Hills, expensive Rodeo Drive and crazy Hollywood. Kevin and Michael are unimpressed and agree "Bob's Place" at home is far more interesting than this gaudy Mecca to self-centered lives. Bob's Place is an Eastern

Shore museum of watermen and hunting memorabilia, a personal collection of a dear friend. The museum is housed in a small building on his property next to the snake shed. From the exterior it appears run down and worn but stepping inside, Bob's Place is a treasure trove of a Chesapeake pioneer, an outdoor life well lived. Antique hunting licenses, ancient crab and eel traps, oyster cans and tongs and hunting gear fill the interior floor to ceiling. Nineteenth century tools used by the ADD warrior then so revered. The gifts of ADD recognized, valued and appreciated by the hunters and pioneers.

Bob is a boy's man, a man's man. Slightly round, with tousled, grey hair and warm friendly brown eyes, Bob is usually seen wearing a green John Deere cap and worn checkered flannel shirt riding his tractor, loving everything about the great outdoors and the Chesapeake Bay. Labrador Retrievers, hunting and fishing are his favorite pastimes and he generously shares these adventures with Michael who thrives under his wing. Bob is a patient caring man who embraces Michael's differences and Michael is eager to learn all there is in Bob's world, a world filled with possibilities and new exploration. Bob is a small miracle and a much appreciated mentor, a true friend who speaks Michael's language.

Kevin and Michael love the freedom that life on the Shore provides, cherishing all that is good about the life we live, languid and intertwined. A summer evening with fresh steamed crabs, Michael's catch of the day caught from our dock. And a brilliant orange, red and purple sunset crosses the bay, like colors being retired for the day; they illuminate the sky, a mere glimpse of the majesty of creation. Why do I feel the need to run, to flee to roads unknown? Or is it just a reprieve from the weight of life with ADD, knowing deep inside I cannot outrun it anyway.

We check into our first real hotel in Santa Monica, luxury I'm unaccustomed to in our travel west, and appreciated all the more by travails throughout. I am so excited Kevin has joined us! I want to jump on the big, lush hotel bed like a school girl on a trampoline. With Kevin here, I relax a little and find myself enveloped in a cocoon in the overstuffed, sumptuous down comforter. And enjoy a much needed afternoon nap, my first siesta on this journey.

Santa Monica is breathtakingly beautiful with sapphire blue skies, rugged mountain landscape and crashing Pacific waves. The birds-eye view of the coastline from the Ferris wheel at Santa Monica Pier is postcard perfect. Sand castle building, dipping our toes in the cool ocean surf, romantic walks on the soft sandy beach, hula pie at Duke's and a rusty old tandem bike ridden on the beach. Reunited, dreams again shared, life is good!

At Third Street Promenade there are ethnic restaurants, a Mecca of trendy shops and street performers. We take in the sights and sounds of the City, listening to the street performers; we are impressed by the variety of talent. Under the bright full moon perched over the ocean we share these simple moments. Moments that defines us with beauty, genuine appreciation and carefree laughter. This is what I long to hear, what truly matters. Family, fleeting irreplaceable moments in time and the best things in life not being things at all! Three thousand miles of lessons echo in my ears.

Road Warrior Wisdom:

* Build in two or three day rest stops at a single location. You need to catch up on sleep and children physically need the time out of the car. It also allows for extra exploration of an area without the rush to push on to the next place.

14

CALIFORNIA DREAMIN'

The life at Malibu Beach enchants me, appearing easy, even carefree; and the ocean whispers sweetly, calling me with the pull of the tide. Mountains breathe and sigh, while deep swollen canyons cascade to a white sandy beach. Seals wallow on the slippery rocks as a fleet of pelicans hover over the ocean surface, ready to dive bomb for food. A school of diving dolphin teems with the limitless expanse of ocean to call home. Is this real or imagined, or trading one plastic life for another? Michael is Scuba certified and has his boater's license, we could live here, escape. But is it really an escape or trying once again to outrun reality? Believing time, distance and maturation could really change anything anyway, ADD is for life. Expectations would surely find us here as well. The geographic cure is never a remedy anyway, Michael and I've tried before and it's as futile as trying to stop the tides. The tide has come in, splashing my white peasant skirt, I do not realize the passage of time while daydreaming, wondering and seeking. The sand castles from earlier have washed away, like the mirage they were, leaving in their place a fresh canvas. An opportunity, for brand new beginnings!

I sign up for a local Ralph's grocery store card and put it on my key chain. A memento to remind me of fresh starts, possibilities and life's realities when I feel lost, overrun by life with ADD and special needs.

Our tandem bike ride to Venice Beach reveals humanity in all its glory! There are people from all walks of life, homeless, dreadlock clad hippies, muscular tan surfers, potheads, yuppies and middle-aged beach bums. A microcosm of life, each with the live and let live philosophy so expressly California! The Venice Boardwalk is a hub of community activity with tee shirt shops, vintage clothing stores and new age boutiques, a feast for our overloaded senses. Posters scream the latest rage . . . war, peace, homosexuality, Jesus and drugs. Everyone's a critic.

The Venice Beach homeless population appears kindred in nature with each person looking out for the next, sharing food, clothing and personal space. We watch a worn woman with crusted eyes, genial missing tooth smile, and wearing a Vote for Pedro tee shirt offer Shorty, a fellow homeless soul, an extra sweater to combat the evening chill, sharing what little she has. A tiny kitten is leashed to a grocery cart, "owned" by a ravaged, weather beaten homeless man wearing three layers of clothes, perhaps all he has. He adopted and feeds the kitten from his own meager food stash collected from garbage cans along the board-walk. Men, women and even children adrift, how does society allow this? Kevin believes them to be houseless not homeless, crafting lives and relationships, just not typical to ours. Not necessarily meaning a poor quality of life, just different. The homeless seem to recognize their utter dependence on one another, a simple trust that crumbs of mercy will happen. Knowing that deep down we all need someone and this hope alone provides the power to live on. Shouldn't I of all people recognize and appreciate difference as a gift? They do appear to enjoy deep and caring friendships, hope and simple joy in daily routine, appearing uncontaminated by society's high expectations. Learning at Venice Beach, when I change the way I look at things, the things I look at change! Perspective, now being everything!

Michael did not venture to Venice Beach with us. His impulsive personality had exploded earlier when asked to turn the television off so others could sleep. Michael is outraged, his Richter Scale off the chart! With everyone now awake. Exhausted from traveling, change in routine and medication, he is overwhelmed! He threatens to leave us and return home however he could. Michael now adrift, is searching frantically for his suitcase, asking for his cash ready to flee. To what or where he doesn't know, not understanding his raging impulse or the dangers that can come from it. A split second decision could change his life forever and it scares me deeply. I am sadly discouraged by his first outburst of the trip. The air emotionally charged with Michael in an unfamiliar urban setting, gone from home so long, angry, frustrated and confused, a vicious cycle of emotions. Without stability and familiarity, he feels disoriented and disconnected which triggers this episode. It's clashing with his need for stability, my homebody at heart, and he is shaken. Kevin, with infinite patience reigning, holds Michael close in a Jaws of Life embrace until he stops trembling. Exhausted from the outburst, Michael settles in to sleep, needing quiet time alone for rest and reflection. Finally seeing his rhythmic breathing steady, Kevin and I go for a walk to regroup. The time alone does him good and soon he rejoins us, welcomed back with open and understanding arms. Arms that have been through crises before, knowing they will come again, but ache to hold him anyway. To make everything all right, for all of us. Doing whatever has to be done to keep our family intact through storms that rage.

As we leave the spectacular Santa Monica beaches, I now daydream of running away. Where no one knows me and I can live in my happily ever after world, alone and pretend. Alone, in a little peaceful cottage by the sea, hibernating with my books, in the comfort of the written word, freed from the weight of disease and disorder. What would my family think? How can I think of hurting the people I most cherish in the world? A Desperate Housewife moment on this road of self discovery.

15

EXTREMES

Through the Mojave Desert passing by the airplane grave-yard, the Suburban rolls into Death Valley National Park, the largest National Park in the continental United States. It sounds treacherous, demanding and desolate and it is. Rattlesnakes call Death Valley home and sandstorms abound. The surprise of the year are blooming delicate wild flowers after an unusually rainy winter. Color and life are unexpected amid the dry cracked desert floor. Birds, reptiles and kangaroo rats traverse the desert plains. Life nestled in, struggling to survive extreme elements, something I know intimately.

The landscape is lunar, with roads appearing endless to the horizon. Your mind plays tricks on you as ghosts and shadows seem to appear in sandstorms and on mountain precipices. Are they aberrations of haunting lost pioneers? Is it a graveyard of disoriented western dreamers or Death Valley Scotty? Ghost towns stand bearing witness to human life and death in this barren, hostile terrain.

A most unexpected sight is the Sierra Nevada Mountains to the west with snow capped mountain peaks! Snow is seen, even as we pass a road sign reading, "Elevation 200 feet Below Sea Level." The temperature in Death Valley is a scorching 114 degrees, hot, but dry winds blow. Borax white sand dunes carved by wind swept ranges and craggy mountainous landscape dominate the desert. Mount Whitney, majestic at 14,000 feet, possesses an immense combination of beauty and danger.

The Furnace Creek Ranch appears like a mirage on the horizon offering an oasis from the relentless heat. Our tiny yellow cabin at the Ranch has a white tin roof to reflect the intense desert heat. The shabby cabin curtains are drawn tight, sealing it from the outside extremes, as a humble window air conditioner struggles to cool the small room, fighting against something so much stronger than it can handle.

Evening, and still 115 degrees in the shade! Swimming in the Furnace Creek Ranch pool for relief causes a strange sensation, feeling cold leaving the pool, a momentary feeling though; in minutes we're fully dry from the dryer like heat. Ice cream's the answer! Ice cream in the desert tastes better than anywhere else in the world, might it be the 115 degrees? We indulge in a double dip each at the sole general store and devour the cool treat. Kevin claims our children are like flavors of ice cream, all different but we love them just the same. We both agree our children's flavors are chocolate, vanilla and rocky road!

The sun sets, a canopy of darkness upon us. The coyote calls to a virtually full moon, shining brightly. A sign outside our cabin warns that mountain lions are nocturnal; and will eagerly seek anything edible left behind. As harsh as Death Valley is, there's tranquility and peace under the star filled sky, stars to the horizon, some as bright as the moon. Our spirits unconfined by a labyrinth of expectations. I realize I need wide-open spaces as much as Michael. A needlepoint pillow resting in a chair at home says it best . . ."Don't Fence Me In."

I rise early and hike to the Devil's Golf Course and Death Valley Visitors Center enjoying the overwhelming silence, the subtle colors and time alone. Warning signs abound, "Beware of Coyotes, Wolves and other Wild Animals" and "Drink Plenty of Water," signs testifying to life and death conditions that are ever-present. I see a wild coyote scrounging for his morning meal and take a wide berth passing by. He's the size of a medium dog with a wolf face and lean angular body, he runs free without ever knowing the gift it is. We depart the blistering land; this is truly the 'wild, wild west.' You can see forever and think clearly here. I see a bumper sticker declaring "All Who Wander Are Not Lost." Amen to that!

We pass through Badwater, the lowest spot on earth, Devils' Corn Field, abandoned mine shafts and fringe towns struggling to survive. The gateway towns to Death Valley are praying for tourist dollars to save them from the same fate as the ghost towns nearby.

We are driving to Sequoia National Park through the lush and fertile San Joaquin Valley. This valley is where most California produce is grown and then quickly shipped, as old box car trains sit in the field awaiting their load, ready for their own cross country travel. We stop at a local roadside stand selling fresh ripe fruits, a bounty right off the vine. Ten varieties of juicy sweet peaches, apricots, plums, plump figs and homemade black licorice are for sale. The colors and shapes are a feast for our desert worn senses. We are famished and eagerly gather a sack full of the exotic fruits. Michael and Christine wash the fruit in a nearby well using a pulley and bucket, working together. We are ravenous for the cool, sweet fruit and eat to our fill, the flavorful sweet juices running down our parched chins.

Sequoia National Park is a jewel of the Sierra Nevada Mountains, a place of astounding natural beauty and the second oldest National Park in the United States. The cool temperature this evening is fifty-eight degrees, quite a contrast to the 115 at Death Valley. We search the car for fleece pullovers and long pants trying to ward off the chill, layering over the thin white tee shirts and cotton khaki camp shorts we've lived in for so long. Traveling from 200 feet below sea level to nearly 8,000 feet above, today, we are journeying through life's extremes.

Sequoia trees are the oldest living things on earth. The first sequoias were saplings when the pyramids in Egypt were being built, giants among men. The General Sherman Tree alone weighs a monstrous 1,300 tons, is 274 feet high and has a base of 103 feet in diameter, enough wood for eighty four homes. It is difficult to grasp the perspective of the tree until we stand next to it, and then, we appear minuscule, insignificant under the great General's glare. Sequoias are fussy trees that thrive in the higher altitude of the Sierra Nevada Mountains. Realizing these trees outlive generations, puts life in perspective. What am I doing with my life and for my children that will bear legacies that outlive me? Will my children even remember how hard I fought for their very survival? What will their adult lives bring, especially with the challenges of ADD/LD and special needs? Questions, always questions, from the road I travel.

After the long and busy day of travel, we finally check in to the Wuksachi Lodge. Michael is thrilled to settle in for the night, exhausted from the dizzy pace of travel. He kicks off his shoes, bounds on the large comfortable bed and reaches for the remote. His day is done, he's crossed the finish line, large and in charge, happy to call it a day. Christine, always seeking the next adventure, is desperate to attend a family campfire puppet show offered by a Park Ranger. Michael makes it clear we should not wait for him as he has no interest in watching puppets dance around a campfire. Two distinct faces of ADD.

Exhausted yet unwilling to send her out in the forest alone, I brave it with her while Kevin too passes on the puppet show, relieved to settle in with Michael and watch TV. Under the canopy of the forest, we gather round as the campfire blazes, with orange and red embers dancing about. The Park Ranger introduces herself and talks about life in the forest, particularly for the large bear population that freely roams the park. She then asks for audience participation to tell the story of the giant Sequoia trees using elaborate puppets and colorful props. Kevin arrives, curious about the campfire program and wondering where we are, and is enchanted to see Christine as part of the show. The Ranger Program turns out to be a very fun and educational event for all three of us! We bask in the warmth and glow of the raging campfire, under a star filled sky, making memories and sharing the sweet simple things in life.

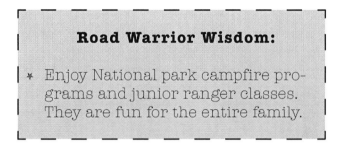

Road Warrior Wisdom:

* Enjoy National park campfire programs and junior ranger classes. They are fun for the entire family.

Sleeping in the cool mountain air, the stars seem close enough to touch. The full moon is the brightest I've ever seen. Is this real or imagined? Or, is this part of a more focused vision for me? My eyes fill with joy in the small things of life; realizing they are the big things after all.

16

HIKE NOW, WORK LATER

Awakened to a surreal blue sky and the silhouette of the dark green ponderosa pines as the mountain tops glisten with snow capped peaks with rays of sunlight like arrows, darting in all directions. Creation appears magnified, and I treasure this moment as a gift.

Michael, rested and refreshed, has hiking clothes on first thing, and we're off to Moro Rock. Climbing Moro Rock is challenging, vertically following a narrow, rickety steel stairway with 400 steps up the steep slippery slope. Christine is the first Nolan to the summit, which irritates Michael again. Pushing past Kevin to stake the claim, now both "boys" shake their heads and shrug their shoulders, realizing once again her competitive nature!

I can see forever on this tiny perch recognizing how a bird must feel when landing on tree tops. I feel small in the process yet large as life itself being privy to such majesty, an awe inspiring view. Snow-covered alpine peaks and Three Rivers' Valley, cars the size of dimes, I am dizzy with possibilities. I am overcome with an awakening, knowing this instant I will never return to society's unreasonably high expectations and accelerated pace. Michael's success will be measured with a new yardstick, freeing him to be exactly who he is meant to be!

We hike four miles to Tokopaw Falls to witness an immense waterfall cascading off a rugged granite face. Bubbling streams below frantically rush off in all directions carving eons of rock along the way. We're alone to see this wonder, watching rascally marmots playing hide and seek, smelling the pine scented air and feeling so alive. A cathedral of nature, I hope Heaven looks like this!

Hiking and mountain climbing continue to be our greatest teacher. So many life lessons are learned, honed and honored on the hiking trail. "Hike now, work later," becomes our favorite saying. Michael carries a Dakine Poacher backpack, looking like a Sherpa ready to summit. It is two sizes too big and Mount Everest ready. Michael stuffs it full each morning ready for any new adventure. Flashlight, an extra trail map, half gallon jug of water, a blanket and compass, he is ready for anything. Ready for life, real life and the joyous adventure a natural life can be. This, from a child who cannot remember homework for his school backpack! Mom, normally a two syllable enunciation for "where's my," as he rushes out the door late for class with hair and clothes askew. School babble, not interesting him the way outdoor hiking adventures do. Lesson after lesson for the ADD Child, and me, comes from the Trails.

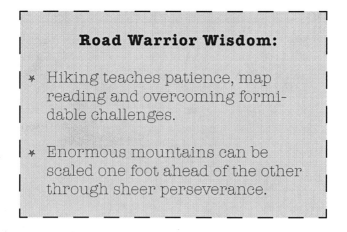

Road Warrior Wisdom:

* Hiking teaches patience, map reading and overcoming formidable challenges.

* Enormous mountains can be scaled one foot ahead of the other through sheer perseverance.

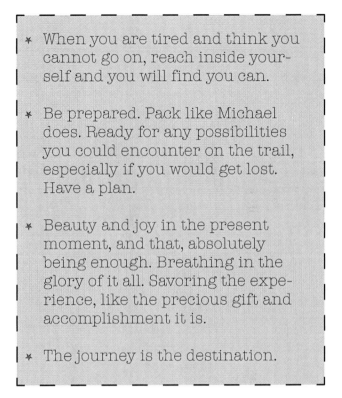

* When you are tired and think you cannot go on, reach inside yourself and you will find you can.

* Be prepared. Pack like Michael does. Ready for any possibilities you could encounter on the trail, especially if you would get lost. Have a plan.

* Beauty and joy in the present moment, and that, absolutely being enough. Breathing in the glory of it all. Savoring the experience, like the precious gift and accomplishment it is.

* The journey is the destination.

Sequoia National Park with trees preserved for generations, sharing tree-ringed tales unmistakably filled with mystic, a spacious and unspoiled place. The park is glorious. A lasting serenity is found in the amazing natural wonders of our spectacular country. Life is not a dress rehearsal; it is the grand performance to be lived now, appreciated and precious, embracing moments without hesitation or reservation. Before the curtain goes down . . . an epiphany, awakening my soul.

A gem, Kings Canyon National Park is located adjacent to Sequoia and turns out to be quite a find. We check into Grant's Grove at the Park and find quaint little cabins built in the 1920's and not updated since. Perfect! The entrance to the cabin is six feet high, Kevin ducks to go in and there are two full sized beds with ancient, frayed bedspreads. It looks like Gulliver's Travels, and now we're the giants in a Lilliputian world. No televisions, no phones, no cell phone service or internet, we are completely unplugged and it's very liberating! We eat a picnic dinner outside on a rusty old table and play checkers on the wide planked floor of the cabin. After dinner we collect twelve inch sugar cone pinecones and watch fireflies twinkle in the crisp mountain air. Life is grand and truly found in the simple things.

Our first bout of altitude sickness! Acute Mountain Sickness (AMS) is manifested by our bodies not being acclimatized to the current altitude. Stomach aches, headaches, shortness of breath and vertigo symptoms as we adjust to the increased altitude, 7,520 feet above sea level with lower oxygen levels. A restless night's sleep as I toss and turn struggling to feel better, trying to calm the illness raging inside, knowing I need all my energy to press on. There is still a long road ahead and the Mothership cannot go down.

17

Roads' End

Thirty-miles into King's Canyon to Roads' End reveals a spectacular landscape and reminds me of the Swiss Alps. The harmonious chorus of "awesome," "ooh's and ah's" and "incredible," are music to my ears until a stray "orgasmic" comes out of Michael, blurting out the first thing he thinks of, his "self talk" valve not working, forever testing my patience. Words truly cannot describe the majesty we see. Framed by glacier carved granite cliffs, virgin forests swell with yucca and aspen trees as well as majestic pines offering a beautiful mantle of color. There may not be a more beautiful place on earth and visiting it rejuvenates my soul.

We meet Joyce, a P. R. Specialist who works for the California Park Service. Joyce is about fifty-five but the years have taken their toll and she looks much older. She has a warm, friendly smile framed by short silver hair. She's a year round resident and eager to share the great wonder of King's Canyon. "Do you need directions? Are you lost?" she asks. The exact question muddling in my mind since I left home and what I hope this trip will answer.

"P. R. Business" she explained is Public Restrooms. Her job is to go to the far reaches of the park and maintain the public bathrooms at trail heads and back country campsites. Her pay had been drastically cut with state cutbacks; she is now per-diem instead of salaried yet still feels so blessed to be in the Park, in the wide-open spaces of this sacred land. Joyce travels daily with a Native American co-worker who has taught her his tribal traditions and customs to view and appreciate "Mother Earth." They routinely stop their sanitation truck at road kill to sprinkle tobacco over the dead creature and bless its soul. She sees with untainted eyes life in hidden places, delights in simplicity, and has surrendered her heart to the rhythm of the land. Michael and Christine are wide-eyed and speechless in the back seat captivated by this random encounter.

King's Canyon is a hidden gem and the park is virtually empty. John Muir, the naturalist of the 1800's says "it rivals Yosemite." In my opinion, it is more spectacular than Yosemite and without the masses of people.

Grizzly Falls is a steep, raging waterfall cascading into the King's River, with powerful white-water that continues to shape Kings Canyon. The American flag flies proudly in the breezy air at the summit of the falls, a symbol so fitting. Kevin and Christine are soaked from the spray of Grizzly Falls, baptized by the beauty of creation, and run high-fiving each other with pure glee, as Michael captures their joy on his video journal. With Michael's dysgraphia, the video journal is a perfect way for him to document his trip.

The sheer majesties of creation continue to astound me. We picnic at Ragging River Falls, serene even with the locomotive sound of the raging cascade. After an hour there, Kevin feels he's been to a meditative spa. Michael and Christine call the picnic lunch the best meal ever. What wonders and perspective the great outdoors bring!

At Road's End, we meet an Australian couple in their seventies, traveling the Western United States on holiday, on a BMW motorcycle they shipped over. I admire their bold journey into the unknowns with two sleeping bags and a cook stove strapped to the back of their bike. They say they will cover two thousand miles over the next month, freedom and adventure on the wide open road. I am inspired to travel like them when I grow up!

It's depressing to leave here. The daydream to flee returns and again I resist its pull. Yosemite National Park waits. And as the crow flies it's nearby but because the Sierra Nevada Mountains are so immense it becomes a 150 mile ride around. No worries partner, it's only driving!

Passing by the massive energy windmills on a hillside, Michael is intrigued. He is documenting ideas and drawing rudimentary pictures in his invention journal, creative and out of the box thoughts are jarred by the strange looking windmills dotting the highway. He wonders where the energy goes, how is it stored, and finally used. Questioning why gasoline for cars, there must be other choices for fuel, the windmills are proof of that. Feverishly making notes, thinking up ideas faster than he can possibly write them down! This is how Michael learns everything best, in a living classroom of Life.

Finally, Fish Camp and clean clothes, we've arrived! The image of fresh clean clothes is something I so took for granted before our travels west. Michael and I find a coin operated washing machine at our motel in Fish Camp and feel like we won the lottery, instantly grateful not to be true pioneers and have to use a barrel and scrub board. Our laundry bag weighs a "ton" and smells like road kill! The bag is relegated to the roof carrier, it is that bad. Michael hoists the bag over his shoulder and together, as a team, we sort, wash, dry, and fold all our clothes; clean again for the first time in two weeks. Ready for a fresh start the little things now more important, even meaningful.

18

FOREST FIRES BURN

Another glorious western morning and I breathe in the beauty, feeling brand-new, now acclimatized to the higher altitude and comfortable. My mind unclogged with minutiae, my thoughts clearer in the wide-open spaces. Am I imagining this? Can this clarity endure once I'm home? I breathe in the sapphire blue skies, cool temperatures, zero humidity and fragrant woodsy pines, like the finest vintage wine.

Yosemite, or "Yo Z mite" as Michael calls it, here we come! John Muir called Yosemite a "temple carved by nature." Our first clue about the massive crowds is a pushy long line entering the park, extending for miles. There is bumper to bumper traffic, tour buses, campers of all sizes and general chaos. I feel like a salmon swimming upstream during spawning season! The congestion seriously distracts from the natural scenic wonder of Yosemite. A small reminder, reminiscent of the hustle and bustle we left behind.

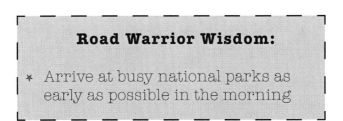

Road Warrior Wisdom:

* Arrive at busy national parks as early as possible in the morning

or late in the afternoon to avoid
crowds. Hiking trails and sights
will be less congested, particularly
at the popular parks.

* An added benefit: wildlife is more
likely to be viewed in the morning
or evening.

El Capitan, Half Dome and the famous Yosemite Falls at 2,425 feet, the second largest falls in the world, are gorgeous sights, with life unfolding before my eyes as they cascade into Yosemite Valley. The Valley, carved by glaciers, is overflowing with spacious wildflower meadows, abundant wildlife and beckoning hiking trails ready for exploration. However, viewing them with others does alter the experience. It seems like the Disneyland of National Parks. I anticipate seeing someone in a moose head costume posing for souvenir photos with the kids. Yosemite is working on the over-crowding issue, and is interested in creating an "in park" shuttle system to eliminate all cars from the park. This would be a good start and has been very successful at Zion National Park in Utah. Yosemite currently utilizes a one-way road system throughout the park to minimize traffic congestion.

We stay at the historic Ahwahnee Hotel, built and opened in the 1927. *Great Lodges of the National Park*s is our template for National Park lodging. The Ahwahnee is a park treasure and a treat to enjoy, also the most expensive of our accommodations. It's a grand and glorious old hotel nestled between Yosemite Falls and the Royal Arches. The rooms are lush and comfortable with old fashioned claw foot bathtubs to soak away our aches from the trail.

Evening hikes at National Parks are an irresistible draw.

Crowds and the hustle bustle of activity are diminished and the wildlife grazes more freely. Kevin and I hike to Mirror Lake using the steep and strenuous horse trail. Michael and Christine cry out that their legs have had enough hiking so a romantic hike for two it is! The lake is a mirrored reflection of the stately peaks, revealing a wonderland of soft mellow reds, yellows and blues, enhanced by the fiery glow of the setting sun. I see an American Bald Eagle, a treasured sight to behold, and a funny family of mule deer is grazing in an open meadow. Stars peek from behind Half Dome to light our way home. As brave rock climbers are suspended in sleeping bags, bedded down for the evening, dangling from the sheer vertical face, their own lanterns a beacon in the dark night sky.

Sleeping in the shadow of the Royal Arches is as restful and peaceful as could be, under the spell of the ancient mountain. At four in the morning, Ashley calls for advice, just barely making her flight to San Francisco. But, a fortunate coincidence to waken at that wee hour, as we witness Mars and the moon travel the night sky together with the red planet aflame. At the higher altitude it seems close enough to touch and is a vision to behold, another random moment in the complexion of time. Living life on life's terms.

The drive leaving Yosemite is less congested than the drive in, allowing us a more relaxing opportunity to appreciate the abundant beauty. Meadows filled with colorful wildflower, ponderosa pines, sheer granite walls carved by glacier ice, and powerful waterfalls fascinate me. We pass a controlled burn section of the park where intentionally set forest fires will allow new growth to root. It seems an odd concept to burn something down, believing it will grow back stronger. Perhaps, this is a metaphor for Michael and me, needing to burn away old routines, habits and ideas about ADD as a curse. Allowing ourselves to be more deeply rooted in the things that matter and for our relationship to emerge from the rubble stronger than before. Emerging out of the smoke covered road, dense as the darkest cave, into a brilliantly clear day I realize how much I'll miss the wilderness as we head to San Francisco. It's where life's most essential lessons speak to me.

Reunited! Ashley arrives, and our family is complete. Like Los Angeles, everyone talks at once, anxious to catch up on these last weeks apart. With Ashley beginning college soon, this time together seems more urgent and precious than ever. Final fleeting seconds to create lasting memories, teach essential life lessons and just bask in the warmth of family. She is in a glorious time of her life, with her road wide open. I sense a push-pull going on inside her. One minute she draws close, young, needy and dependent and then pushing as far away as she can, fiercely strong and independent.

San Francisco is an exciting and vibrant city teeming with life. Fisherman's Wharf, Alcatraz Island, shopping at Pier 39 and Chinatown, a patchwork of urban living, woven together like a work of art. The fog moves with a life of its own, like rolling waves from the Pacific Ocean, the city encapsulated under its spell. The Golden Gate Bridge peers out of the fog, with its brilliant orange hue playing peek-a-boo with the city. Alcatraz Island haunts and screams to be remembered as silhouettes of prisoners long gone look searchingly out collapsed cell windows at freedoms lost. The chill in the air felt to the bone. Fisherman's Wharf street performers captivate tourists, entertaining with music, magic and mime, to chase their share of the abundant tourist dollars. We walk Rice-a-Roni Hill and the Crooked Street, talking endlessly and eating our fill of Ghirardelli chocolate, enjoying all that San Francisco has to offer. The city is complex and multifaceted.

Hiking is hiking no matter the terrain and lessons from the trail are nearly the same. To Chinatown, sixteen blocks due north up the steep winding trademark San Francisco streets. Map in hand we're off, Christine and I leading the charge like drill sergeants. Brilliant red lanterns with bright beads hang on the street lamps and Chinese lettered street signs tell us we've arrived. Chinatown boasts the largest Chinese population in the United States and it's a culture Chinese-Americans are proud of, as the signs of restaurants and shops proclaim.

Imitation *Chanel, Louis Vuitton* sunglasses, handbags and dozens of unusual shops make Chinatown a treasure hunt. The grocery stores and apothecaries are fascinating too, filled with an array of different foods and peculiar medicines. Peking ducks, dead or alive depending on the customer's preference, herbs, teas and roots can be purchased there. The children are wide-eyed, their heads darting around in all directions seeing unfamiliar sights, trying to absorb this foreign land.

Michael is searching for Samurai swords in exotic Chinatown. Weapons equal power and control, something he thinks he can buy. Not recognizing his own power within, buried with his self-esteem, diminished by his personal struggles in an unfriendly world of expectations, unable to be met. The swords gleam with sharp, threatening blades exposed for all to fear and revere. Presumably they are for display purposes only as the wooden racks suggest. However, in Michael's ADD/LD world they scream power and control, a way out of invisibility. This thinking scares me and I leave the store angry and brooding that he doesn't see it my way, after all I have his best interests at heart. We're locked in a contest of wills, our magnets again pushing each other away, with our old tapes replaying the same show. Michael is angry, disappointed and fixated on the swords, arguing that the girls are buying handbags, valuing them the same as the Samurai swords he covets. Speaking different languages once again, we need an interpreter to settle this avalanche of emotions careening out of control before we're engulfed and cannot find a way out; losing the precious ground of growth we've covered these many miles. Kevin in his patient and diplomatic way, steps in to calm our storm. We find our way back to each other without crisis. On the streets of San Francisco we make peace, agreeing to disagree over weaponry. Michael announces, "I will sleep on it." And that's the end of the Samurai Swords, for now.

Monitoring teenagers is always necessary but a teenager with ADD especially needs well defined, consistent black and white boundaries. Their impulsiveness, natural curiosity and fearlessness are a dangerous combination with hormones raging. But, they do need to be acknowledged, to know their voices are heard, and to know they're respected and understood. Often the ADD Child is isolated and alone, feeling as though they are invisible, believing peers and society look right through them as though they don't exist. Their reputations are hard to get out from under so new social progress is slow. Friendships are a challenge to make and maintain, yet the ADD teenager is desperate for personal contact, seeking and needing inclusion, a sense of belonging. Isolated and excluded by ADD is far more dangerous than any weapon.

Famished by the strenuous walk and Samurai swords, we enjoy the infamous Boudin sourdough bread bowl chowder and Dungeness crab cocktails beside a cozy, outdoor waterfront fire. Sourdough bread is trademark San Francisco; indulging, we couldn't help sending some back home to family and friends. I cherish my family of five realizing how quickly time is passing, and how precious these moments are, memories for a lifetime, swords and all! Will they remember this moment and treasure the carefree family laughter and joy I feel right now? And know these are the only moments that really matter after all.

19

Now we are Nine

The morning fog again rolls in, an eerie sight, as it moves with a life of its own. Wrapping the city in its web and concealing its secrets. Ashley gathers food for breakfast to feed homeless men and women living around Fisherman's Wharf. She gathers her brother and sister as well, and heads out with her pink tote filled with cereal, fruit, juice boxes and croissants. It is a beautiful sight witnessing their compassion for humanity, feeding societies neediest, a bright light to these less fortunate souls. Their worn faces with cracked lips, tired vacant eyes, stooped postures of dependency and matted hair do not frighten the children; hungry for more than food, they are also grateful for compassionate personal contact and respect. I watch from a distance and am reminded of the Starfish story. A man walking along a beach was tossing starfish back into the water, one by one while another man asks "how can that possibly make a difference, the ocean and beach are so vast?" The man holding a single starfish tossed it into the ocean saying, 'I made a difference for that one." One, each one can reach one. The children reaching out and acknowledging each as a person, singular and unique, not forgotten. Just like the ADD child, one at a time, with time, patience and attention, we can make a difference. A glorious moment I will never forget. I am astounded by the depth of their sensitivity and realize in that instant, my legacy will live on. Like the giant sequoias.

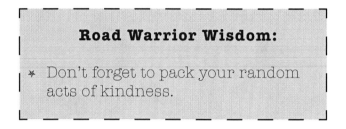

Road Warrior Wisdom:

* Don't forget to pack your random acts of kindness.

Now we are nine! Tracy and her family arrive to join us. She and her husband, Bruce, share our love of the great outdoors, our quest for new states, National Park wonders and road warrior fun. The cousins scream to see each other, fellow compatriots on this crazed journey. Our families fit together well for road warrior travel. This, our second summer west and numerous other weekends attest to road warrior worthiness. They're not intimidated by the challenges of ADD and offer unconditional love and support, appreciating the gifts of ADD, sensitivity, compassion, wonder and fearlessness for whatever comes along.

Bruce is patient, quiet and easy going, much like Kevin. He too, traveled west as a child crossing similar terrain. Bruce loves the wide open West, a kindred spirit, always up for any adventure. He is a saint with Michael, sharing a brilliant mind for geology, intrepid hiking skills and western fun, all the things Michael likes best.

Our children are best friends, having spent a lot of time together. From cribs to college, they have been close friends and travel companions. Michael and Jeff, two months apart in age, are more like brothers. Jeff is quiet and introspective much like his father. He has an innate ability to watch the world around him in a non-judgmental way, rolling through life with ease. Michael and Jeff share a strong bond: he is the one true friend Michael has ever known. Lindsay, their youngest, is a teenaged drama queen. You know she and Christine are related! Lindsay, like most teenagers, is in the wanting to be "coo" stage, cool for us Neanderthals. She looks up to Ashley and tolerates Christine. Lindsay has a broken collar bone from falling off a hammock two days ago so her activities are limited. She has a big smile despite the pain and is glad to join the fray knowing there's adventure ahead.

Tracy and I are tucked in bed in our pajamas having our own slumber party like ten-year-old giddy girls sharing "boy crush" secrets. We are downloading photographs from the trip, needing bifocal glasses to see, and catching up on news, old news, new news, and most importantly sister news. Sister secrets shared from the heart. Ashley glances over at our giggles and wonders what teenage pajama party she has crashed.

Westward Ho for our family of nine! All the "pioneers" ready to go, our covered wagon style caravan leaves for Oregon tomorrow.

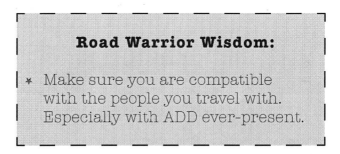

Road Warrior Wisdom:

* Make sure you are compatible with the people you travel with. Especially with ADD ever-present.

We are on the road again, leaving California and heading north to the wilds of Oregon. Following caravan style with two-way radios gives us a feeling of traveling together. We use the radios regularly to communicate messages, direction of travel and commentary on sights we see. Michael, resourceful as ever on long trips, and with a good sense of humor, turns the radio into a personal microphone entertaining our caravan with moose "rap" over the airway. The spontaneously funny song has us in stitches, until suddenly a gruff angry voice appears, abruptly ending his show. Life lived on the road with an ADD kid and a crotchety world filled with expectations.

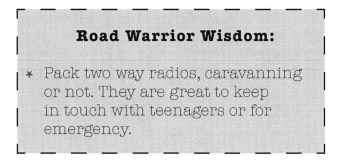

Road Warrior Wisdom:

* Pack two way radios, caravanning or not. They are great to keep in touch with teenagers or for emergency.

We detour to Lassen Volcanic National Park, established after an eruption in 1915. Entering the park, we immediately see snow! Amidst the snow are boiling sulphur pits, active geo-thermic activity at Bumpus Hill and volcanic rock debris strewn like buoyant bath toys. Mt. Shasta, a 10,000 foot peak in the distance, majestically reigns over this surreal sight. There are snow drifts taller than my car, remnants of a harsh winter and an invitation for a summer snowball battle.

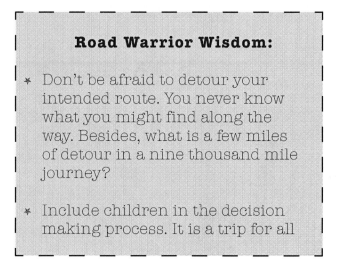

Road Warrior Wisdom:

* Don't be afraid to detour your intended route. You never know what you might find along the way. Besides, what is a few miles of detour in a nine thousand mile journey?

* Include children in the decision making process. It is a trip for all

Michael boils over and I'm caught off guard by the sudden shift from carefree laughter and fun, to anger. Michael reverts to before trip behavior of taunting and bullying Christine for effect. Just 24 hours since my sister's family joined us, all the excitement is hard for him to contain, and rarely in ADD does it manifest itself in a positive manner. Realizing that is where the regression comes from when he has been doing so well. One giant step forward comes with a few steps back. This is ADD!

Michael pounds Christine with snowballs. Defenseless against his barrage she reaches for her greatest weapon, her Daddy! Daddy will save her and save her he does, coming to her rescue like a knight in shining armor. Kevin too, discouraged by his loss of control. He joins the snowball battle and it's soon over, Michael defeated in the snowy slope, covered in the cold, wet snow he cruelly rained on Christine. Michael snarls, angry at the world and perhaps embarrassed and disappointed in himself. Shockingly, he appears surprised at the outcome, as though it was unexpected. Awkwardness reigns as Michael's behavior and impulsive outburst cause a rift. Out of the snow packed rubble he crawls, regretful of his behavior, and reluctantly apologizes to Christine. Forgiveness for Michael once again, and with my own crumbled heart, Kevin and I reassure him that it is over and all is not lost. Again testing the theory that what doesn't kill us makes us stronger! Leaving Lassen, the snow, and Michael's frustration behind, we press on. Miles to go and still learning my way, the road never as clear as I think.

Cell phone service is virtually nonexistent in the mountains, yet Ashley copes well. She does however; have her laptop computer plugged into an inverter and downloads photos from an hour earlier, a twenty-first century woman through and through. I wonder aloud, what her trip West will look like when she is my age, a fourth generation to go West seeking answers? She assures me she will not be having a breakdown at forty-five and will be flying wherever she needs to go. Oh to be young again!

A scrumptious Mexican dinner in Weed, California, no I'm not kidding! The teenagers think this is very funny and cannot wait to report us to their friends. A testament to the fact that yes indeed, their parent's have lost it or maybe never had it, a scarier thought indeed. Mount Shasta reigns over Weed with an unexpected grandeur as we bask in the orange and red glow of the luminescent sunset.

Tracy's face is memorable when she sees the chain motel I book in Klamath Falls, Oregon, truck stop, motorcycle rally and all. It is July 4th weekend and I am not a miracle worker. Pushing on from Weed without reservations we suddenly feel compelled to have something certain and these rooms, according to a dozen calls during dinner, are the only two rooms for the next 200 miles. The adults discuss, "How do nine people sleep in two cars if we don't take the rooms?" Ashley instantly perks upon overhearing this conversation, "Could this wilderness trip get any worse?" Michael and Jeff scream "yes" to camping out which sounds like a great plan to them, until that is, it is pitch dark and they are the ones outside the cars!

Road Warrior Wisdom:

* Pack a tent and sleeping bags, just in case. I wish we had a tent to camp in National Park campsites.

* Don't miss the chance of a lifetime to sleep under the stars!

Michael's Mom

> * Any opportunity for family time
>   around the campfire is priceless.

The motel is clean and a place to sleep which is all we need to break up the long drive to Crater Lake. The woman at the front desk is the nicest motel clerk I've met. She has blazing red hair, bright blue eyes and chatters a mile a minute. She wants to share everything about the motel amenities including a hot tub, which has no takers. Another weary traveler trying to get a room at the sold out motel is turned away with her perky advice, "If you go to a no-name motel, check the room before you pay." Tracy is shocked when I assure her this is exactly the type of place I stay when traveling west alone and is perfectly safe. I'm not sure she slept a wink last night knowing our sole source of security was the flimsy chain across the door. Life lived on life's own terms.

20

CRATER LAKE BLUE

The girls are in the Chief, the Suburban's nickname, named for the antique wooden cigar store Indian, purchased as a souvenir from Cody, Wyoming last summer. The children marveled at the horizontally packed six foot "Chief" taking half the precious car space thinking once again I had lost it. With two thousand miles to travel home and seeing the proud "Chief" so carefully packed and padded, they were instantly inspired to rename the car. The "Chief" took on personality and came to life on the long trip home, becoming one of the intrepid travelers and survivors of Trip West One. He gallantly guards our family room and reminds me everyday of the potential the West holds.

Road Warrior Wisdom:

* Allow room for Souvenirs!

A short drive north and we're at Crater Lake National Park, the only National Park in Oregon. We are unanimous! This is the most beautiful spot on Earth. A panoramic sight of Crater Lake reveals the bluest blue I've ever seen, so blue, the Oregon sky appears grey. Crater Lake is the second deepest lake in North America, at 1,932 feet, causing this color phenomenon. Routinely, developed film was returned with an apology for overexposing the colors when actually the blue is that intense. Even from a plane at 30,000 feet the rich blue shade is noticeably unique. The crater of Crater Lake is the only remaining evidence of a volcanic eruption more than 7,000 years ago. The eruption was so cataclysmic in scale it imploded a mountain and could be seen as far as Nebraska. There is also archeological evidence suggesting the presence of Native Americans.

We stay at the restored Crater Lake Lodge, a beautiful National Park inn perched on the rim of the crater. It has a mere seventy one rooms and is open from May to October. It's adorned with hand carved hemlock trim throughout, with a wide veranda on the crater side with ancient wicker rockers made of willow to while away the day. Checker boards grace various tables for amusement before lunch.

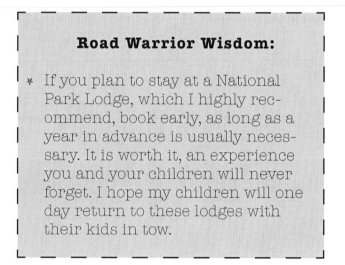

Road Warrior Wisdom:

∗ If you plan to stay at a National Park Lodge, which I highly recommend, book early, as long as a year in advance is usually necessary. It is worth it, an experience you and your children will never forget. I hope my children will one day return to these lodges with their kids in tow.

To work off lunch, we hike Garfield Peak Trail, a strenuous hike to the rim of the crater. It is a challenging hike on gravel and rock along steep narrow switchbacks to reveal a magnificent view of blue Crater Lake. The lake is crystal clear, fed only by the 500 inch annual snowfall and frequent rain. Kevin, Michael, Christine, Jeff and I are the most intrepid hikers today, hiking to the top where a trail marker temporarily blocks the rest of the trail from three feet of fresh spring snow. Good hearted snowball fun now ensues, the lesson from Lassen still fresh. Michael and Christine beg to disobey the sign and continue hiking through the snow to the rim. Fearless, ready, and first! We make them obey the Trail Closed sign, unwilling to chance injury or accident on the steep snowy trail. Once again reminding Michael and Christine that rules are for a good reason and for everyone's safety, they don't have to like them but they must obey them. Always, why, why, why . . . ADD challenging the rules, spontaneously focused on the perceived fun and adventure and unable to process the potential consequences of fun gone bad.

A thirty three mile drive around the rim reveals the volcano carved landscapes. Phantom ship is a craggy mountainous island resembling a lost vessel, almost an aberration appearing from nowhere, floating in the crystal blue lake. Wizard Island is a crater within the crater and the Pinnacles are ash hoodoos where the volcano vented its blistering steam lingering after the eruption. Mount Scott is an interesting sight too, watching snowboarders without the convenience of chair lifts hiking up the mountain for that one thrilling run down the snow covered slope, in July!

Christine earns a Junior Ranger Badge through the park program. She is beaming with pride putting her heart fully into the effort. National Park Rangers are incredibly dedicated people. The familiar brown hats are a friendly park sight. They inspire us to live life outside the box and teach and train current and future generations to defend National Park resources, and appreciate them as the great treasure they are. Meeting these young men and women who love the great outdoors and cherish the adventures inherent in parks, I can see Michael here. I am always on the lookout for where he fits working to make his dreams once again, a reality.

Push-Pull . . . Ashley is tired, irritable and collapsing under the weight of isolation. She's a city girl who loves the excitement, variety, and busyness of nightlife. City smells and sounds rejuvenate her, give her energy and feed her spirit. Ashley does not share my love of the wilderness. She despises the isolation, getting dirty and ostensibly, nothing to do. I rub her back as she lies in bed crying. A soothing mother's touch, she eventually falls asleep, her breathing steady and calm yet her spirit still restless.

Christine wakes me at midnight to see the night sky knowing I love star filled skies. The galaxy reveals the most stars I've seen on a single night in a single place! Stars even to the horizon and seemingly close enough to touch. The black Oregon sky shone the brightest stars and without city smog or lights it is an intense show. There are four shooting stars in five minutes, the radiant Milky Way and storied constellations traverse the heavens presenting a canopy of ageless possibility. I learn at a park lecture that the same stars we see at night are out during the day, you just cannot see them. But they are there watching over us, the miracle that they are, and I am comforted by this thought.

This is real life, what I hoped to see, feel and live when this journey began weeks ago. Why, I wonder, is life ever called ordinary? And why, did I even think I wanted normal?

21

VAST AND UNTAMED

Independence Day, July 4th. I wake before dawn to watch the sunrise over Crater Lake. I wrap myself in a woolen blanket since the evening chill lingers and wait and watch, breathing in the promise of a new day. Morning mist is rising from the lake as a lone star is retiring across the western sky and dawn peers over the eastern horizon. A silent sliver of fiery red finally claims the day as its own, slowly making it authority known, its powerful presence felt. It's glorious, peaceful, and spiritual viewing the resplendence of a single new day, one day, one moment, a microcosm. I am filled with a reverence that makes me want to fall to my knees, another miracle on the road less traveled. The reds, oranges and yellows are a feast for my senses as shadows dance over Wizard Island, the primordial rocks glowing with life. I am awed and humbled by this magnificent sight.

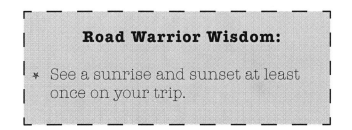

Road Warrior Wisdom:

* See a sunrise and sunset at least once on your trip.

Refreshed by the enchantment of the sunrise, we're off for a morning hike on Cleetwood Cove Trail, my hiking boots laced on first thing. No rest for the weary. I will sleep when I am home, returned to my predictable life. I will miss life on the road, the west and wide-open spaces. Confinement is difficult, "Don't Fence Me In" to societal constraints, mean, superficial and petty people, schedules, color coding, quest for perfection and fitting in. These are all the things I am letting go, freeing myself of the need to do or be anything other than me. Permission granted as I find myself in the glory of the moment.

Bruce calls Cleetwood Cove Trail a "highlight of his life." The trail is a reverse hike, one mile descending from the rim of the Crater to the Lake and returning on steep switchbacks to the rim. We hike along the craggy rock strewn shoreline and dip our tired dusty feet in the freezing waters marveling at the moment. Splashing my weary feet in the frigid water, I sense promise. The ascent up the narrow gravel trail leaves us breathless; it feels like a seventy story climb! Taking in the last of Crater Lake, color, sights and sounds feels urgent. You can go far and wide and never see a sight so breathtakingly gorgeous. This is what I imagine Heaven will look like, peaceful and tranquil, with the bluest blues, crystal clear lakes, snow capped mountain peaks, and sunlight harmoniously dancing around.

Bruce, with the patience of a saint, cheers Michael up the last leg of the hike, encouraging his every step as Michael swears he can't go on, breathless and exhausted by the climb. Bruce, at his side on the slow ascent is his biggest cheerleader, pulling up the rear together one single step at a time, cheering Michael on. Conqueror's indeed! The intrepid hikers pose for a Kodak moment, beaming at their accomplishment . . . perseverance and fortitude wrapped in unconditional love, the lessons learned on Cleetwood Cove.

It is hard to leave but we must go. I depart with a feeling of loss, leaving something of myself behind in the vast untamed kaleidoscope of immaculate beauty that is Crater Lake. Maybe that is really me at the core, untamed with an all consuming desire to roam and appreciate the beautiful nooks and crannies of God's creation, experiencing singular moments that seem so lost in the survival of the day to day mayhem of life with ADD.

We are traveling to Mount Hood, Oregon through varied terrain, from foothills to timberline to tundra. We pass by the Three Sisters Mountain range, imposing Mount Jefferson, desert land forms, black lava beds and lush forests with many shades of green.

Ashley continues to be sullen since this is not the Ritz vacation she had in mind and is second guessing her decision to join us. She pushes away from us sensing more differences than similarities. Desiring something different for her summer fun, yet cooperating and trying to make the best of it, she keeps with the scheduled itinerary. On the cusp of young adulthood she sits.

The historic Timberline Lodge, built in 1936 at the height of the Great Depression is our overnight stop and one of the few lodges open all four seasons. The stunning Cascadian architecture of the hotel is most obvious in the hand wrought iron work, carved wooden staircases and a round two story fireplace that welcomes guests. A multi-paned floor to ceiling window offers a panoramic view of regal Mount Hood, a slumbering volcano and Oregon's highest peak. Lunch is enjoyed in the historic Cascade Dining Room served by a cute and perky young waitress named Spirit. Why does that name sound so Oregonian? Our legs are worn-out after the Cleetwood Cove Trail, so the pool is perfect for the rest and relaxation we all desperately need, kid friendly fun times nine! Good hearted rough housing ensues, a necessary release after a long day on the road.

The hotel is famous for its exterior appearance in the thriller, *The Shining*. Tonight is movie night at Timberline Lodge and what's showing, *The Shining*, of course. Too scary for me and one by one our group of nine fades from the theater. The stars outside are disappointing as well, after the magnificent light show of Crater Lake. I feel a change happening in me, please let it be lasting.

22

CHASING WINTER

Awakened at dawn by the sound of clomping ski boots, it feels like a dream. July 5th and the ski slopes on Mount Hood open at 7:00 a.m. Tracy and I are like little kids on Christmas morning, awake early, dressed in our ski clothes and ready to go skiing NOW. It's an out of body experience to ski in July. I wake my family with a hurry up, let's go skiing cry!

Michael, to my dismay decides not to ski. Despite my enthusiastic attempts to get him on the slopes, he says, no. I am confused by his reply since Michael is our best skier and happiest on the slopes where his fearless ADD spirit runs free, usually the first one out in the morning and the last one in at night, always seeking one more thrilling run. I secretly dream he will join National Ski Patrol one day, again on the lookout for career possibilities. What I learn later, is Mount Hood looks daunting to ski and he fears failure so publicly, accustomed to failure yet still fearful of it, the ever elusive success seemingly just out of his grasp. This is the heart breaking struggle of ADD. Realizing I must let it go for now, and free him from the bondage of my expectations, it is with a new heart that I walk away, giving up my expectations for this picture perfect family outing.

Ashley is absolutely in for this great adventure even if only for the photographic proof and bragging rights she will enjoy later.

Christine, who also skies fearlessly, charges ahead, "First Nolan on the chairlift," she screams as she makes her way through the crowds. We join the girls for this carefree fun, thrilled by the uniqueness of it. Together we feel we're conquering Everest and our enthusiasm is great.

Mount Hood looks like the surface of the moon with snow, rocks and rugged craters. The resort altitude is 8,500 feet with 1,500 feet vertical open. It's an exhilarating feeling to be on snow skis, wearing shorts! Endorphins are on overload. There are no lift lines so ski runs are numerous. We ski the entire morning with abandon and great joy, shushing down the slopes, free as can be. Complimentary snow cones at the base with summer sunshine and wild flowers in glorious bloom make for a fitting end. Chasing winter on a summer day!

Our caravan travels north, so much to see, so little time. We cross the Columbia River, Lewis and Clark's passage to the Pacific Ocean. I picture them so clearly with Sacagawea and her baby Pomp on the dugout canoes saying "Westward Ho," and feeling the salty spray of the Pacific Ocean realizing they had made it. My own pioneer travels seem so inconsequential but are born of the same spirit. I no longer fight the feeling; instead I now embrace it, not allowing my spirited wandering self to be hidden by disguise but to freely roam. The girl in the mirror is someone I recognize.

Welcome to Washington, a "new state." We pass Mount Saint Helens and the active volcano looks sinister. The May 18, 1980 eruption of Mount Saint Helens caused loss of life, decimated trees and forests and ended most area recreation. The summit of the mountain was lowered 1,300 feet in the violent explosion. Wildlife gone, the ebb and flow of life and land altered by an unexpected event. Recently amidst the devastation, renewal is occurring as trees, plants and wildlife are attempting to reclaim the lost land. Yet steam and gases are again venting from the mountaintop, dark, menacing and angry, the aberration appears. The geologists are on high alert as this sleeping volcano has awoken, expecting an eruption to be imminent, knowing it's only a matter of time. Push-pull, as new life also stakes a claim.

The "shortcut" road we travel, feels like life with ADD. Hairpin turns, then straightway only to be surprised by another switchback. And on and on the road twists and turns. It is one hundred miles long and there is no reprieve from the roller coaster feeling, the road keeps my stomach in knots. The dense forest surrounding us does not seem to offer a way out. We slow down; speed up—never maintaining a consistent speed, never a no-wake zone on the ADD style road.

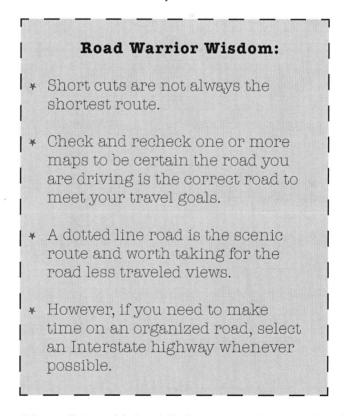

Road Warrior Wisdom:

* Short cuts are not always the shortest route.

* Check and recheck one or more maps to be certain the road you are driving is the correct road to meet your travel goals.

* A dotted line road is the scenic route and worth taking for the road less traveled views.

* However, if you need to make time on an organized road, select an Interstate highway whenever possible.

Mount Rainier National Park is our tenth national park of this journey. The mountain is an awe-inspiring 14,000 foot peak, the highest in Washington State and another sleeping volcano. It dominates the view for hundreds of miles. Today we only glimpse its majesty, since it's mysteriously shrouded in Pacific fog nine days out of ten. Our first stop, Christine Falls is for a photo opportunity for Christine, who beams at being there, proudly sprawling in front of the sign that proclaims her name. Michael again shrugs, sisters! Silvery rushing falls tumble from the melting snow above. A stone bridge traverses the terrain cutting a path for visitors to enjoy the falls up close. The spray brings a chill to our bones in the damp foggy air. We attempt a family Christmas card photograph at the falls but are shell-shocked from the tumultuous road we drove. Vulnerable, wind blown and exhausted by the struggles of the road! Michael appears aloof, standing alone several feet away, appearing alone as the shot is taken. Reminding me once again of what family life with ADD feels like, what a lonely harrowing road it is.

We stay at Paradise Lodge in Paradise, built in the 1910's, another historic park inn. The Lodge is closed in winter, buried under sixty feet of snow, so this is a special time to enjoy the inn's brief life. The Lodge is a charming old cedar structure with the unusual oddity of shared hall baths and showers. Grand raging fireplaces with squirrel shaped wrought irons, still necessary in the damp summer chill to warm visitors. The parchment shades dangling from the three story lobby are hand painted with local wildflower motifs. Paradise found.

Michael and Jeff, without television as a distraction, amuse themselves with old-fashioned checkers and card games by the fire. A Park Ranger is conducting a presentation on pioneer women in Mount Rainier Park, so Christine and I are all ears. Michael, thinking this program compares to the puppet show, continues with his checker game. These early female adventurers climbed the 14,000 foot summit of Mount Rainier in fourteen days. Wearing long dresses! Spirited and strong-willed women of the early 1900's, whose genetics Christine and I so clearly share. Their own voices screamed inside, were heard, understood and acted upon, despite Victorian society's strict mandates.

The rain on the wooden roof lulls me to sleep as the mountain slumbers under a heavy blanket of fog. The fog is like a cocoon, opaque and still, encapsulating my soul, and transforming my heart. My pioneer spirit feels alive here. Dreams and possibilities seem endless.

23

CONESTOGA WAGON TRAIN

The morning fog lifts like a stage curtain, revealing colorful wild flowers in riotous bloom. Mount Rainier receives significant and routine rainfall, making it feel like a terrarium. The ground and trees are moss covered with lush, dense forests with varying shades of green from the moist air. A feast for my already overloaded senses! What will be remembered from this adventure? How will we be changed? What will we take home? Have the forest fires cleansed our souls and consumed the old dead brush, made us new, fresh, and ready to grow.

A long day of travel ahead and the children are all out of sorts, having been in too many places in too few days. We decide to split the boys and girls up, literally. All girls, moms included, are riding in the Chief and the boys, dads included, are in the Trail Blazer. We intend to cover the 600 miles to Canada today with nine people in tow. Not a simple task with three travelers in one car much less nine in two cars, an ambitious feat, but do it we will!

We entertain ourselves in the Chief with typical girl fun. Chattering and yakking a mile a minute, yoga, car exercises we make up, journal writing, shopping lists, doodling fashion designs and singing Camp Oneka songs. The boys, on the other hand, making their way in the Trail Blazer, are having their own little fraternity party. Loud rock music, body noises, jokes I am sure we're glad to miss, swimsuit issues, wishful thinking of dream girlfriends, and shoes removed as they settle in, as though ready for the "big game." The testosterone is raging, and Michael is so grateful for a car full of it, always being outnumbered by the girls. Making a quick rest stop at the halfway point, we greet each other again, the Chief smelling of sweet perfume and the Blazer like a locker room! This division of the sexes appears to have saved the day, and spirits again soar, possibilities endless. Loaded back in, we hit the trail ready to conquer the roads once again.

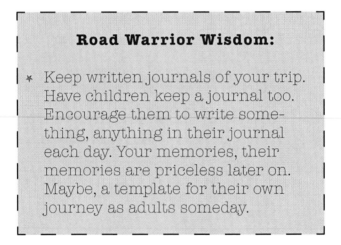

Road Warrior Wisdom:

* Keep written journals of your trip. Have children keep a journal too. Encourage them to write something, anything in their journal each day. Your memories, their memories are priceless later on. Maybe, a template for their own journey as adults someday.

We stop for a well deserved and much needed dinner break at the Panhandle Diner in Bonner's Ferry, Idaho for the blue plate special, which we devour. The final decision is made to push on to Lake Louise. That gives us a solid three day stay at Lake Louise, an extended break from the road we desperately seem to need. Crossing into Canada, we clear the International Border Checkpoint, reminding Michael, "no antics!" Border officials do not have a sense of humor for ADD related wisecracks. Ashley is frantically making her last few phone calls to the civilized world of friends and boyfriend, before her cell phone service goes kaput. A teenager unplugged from civilized society in these far-flung places, Ashley daydreams of fleeing these crazy nomads. Her smile is fading under the weight of the trip. Surely the police will understand her plight, her need to flee to the civilized and "normal" world.

Our first stop for gas in Yahk, British Columbia, makes Michael's list of strange named towns. We are sure we have spent too many hours on the road when we see a family of goats on the roof of a house! Live baby goats trained by an eleven-year-old girl to graze for grass she grew on her roof. We laugh ourselves silly, punchy from the long miles, while Michael captures the sight on his video journal, the wheels turning in his head. I instantly wonder what brilliant idea he could possibly have in mind for our house when we return.

It's a strange feeling today, heading due east for the first time since I left home. I feel the pull of home and it scares me, am I ready? Have I learned what I needed to learn? And are the lessons eternal or fleeting? Will this change the path for Michael and me through the dark woods of ADD?

Kootenay National Park is a jewel of the Canadian Rocky Mountains. Abundant wild animals abound including an impressive big horn sheep, which we nearly hit entering the park! There are many species that make their home at Kootenay, elk, mule deer and pronghorn antelope which also freely roam. Glacier carved canyons, salt infused hot springs and Bryce Canyon styled red hoodoos' make up the park landscape. In the twilight, the Rockies rise like an impassable barrier with broad U-shaped valleys and the ice-carved land captivating in the setting sun.

It is 10:00 p.m. Mountain Time and still light outside. In the summer months, the average daylight at this latitude is seventeen hours. The radiant twilight makes the long drive more manageable, as we miscalculated the drive by sixty arduous miles. Driving the very windy road through Kootenay National Park, and struggling not to hit wildlife slows our progress significantly, with the children now as exhausted and battered as the road.

We finally arrive at Paradise Bungalows in Lake Louise at 10:30 . . . fourteen hours after our morning departure. It is dusk outside and we are ravaged, weary travelers; you would think we crossed these Canadian Rocky Mountains in horse drawn Conestoga wagons. We are way out of our comfort zones on the road this long. I shower the day off at midnight wondering if we, if I, can go the distance.

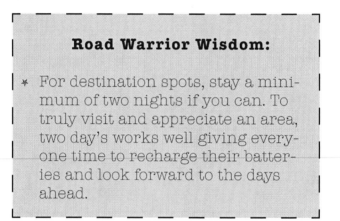

Road Warrior Wisdom:

* For destination spots, stay a minimum of two nights if you can. To truly visit and appreciate an area, two day's works well giving everyone time to recharge their batteries and look forward to the days ahead.

Michael's Mom

24

THANKFULNESS

What a difference a good night's sleep makes! It is an exhilarating feeling to wake up and know we're in the same spot for the next two days. My world so small in some ways: the Suburban, a reusable water bottle, check in-check out, a toothbrush and a change of clothes are all I need. My grey roots are creeping out and my windblown, desert dry hair resembles the business end of a mop! You would think I am a vagabond living a life of such monastic simplicity.

But, where my world has been so greatly touched is in the absolute knowledge of God's glorious creation, and Michael's and my place in it, and how much can be accomplished when embracing ADD as a gift and not a curse. I have heard the overwhelming noise in my life, having been lost in the seduction of consumption, in the tyranny of the urgent and instant gratification; finding counterfeit places within. Superficial dreams are being replaced by realistic dreams and expectations for me and for my family. Freedom from life always orchestrated, without spontaneity and simple joy filled moments. I have learned how loud stillness and silence can speak—blessings from the road.

I once believed this would be a pilot trip for a "round the world" journey. A hands on home schooled adventure I dreamed for Michael. I have an over-stuffed canvas bag at home with travel guides, a book, *1,000 Places To See Before You Die*, how-to books and personal journals of round the world travel. I sometimes escape to the stories of adventure, just like when I was a girl sitting at my grandparent's feet listening to the travel wonders they so richly shared. I feel alive and hopeful once again in the wanderlust inherent on the open road. Now, certain at this crossroad we are not ready for round the world travel, the language of disorders seems like foreign country enough and maybe that introspection is enough. Dreams remain though, providing hope.

Shopping at Lake Louise Village, civilization, and Ashley is smiling! The randomness of shopping offers relief and a sense of the ordinary, following routine and familiar aspects of daily life. Grocery shopping for our picnic dinner becomes a currency lesson as the children struggle to compute the currency exchange! Michael asks if they take "American money," and eyes the strange looking dollars he gets as change. A good math lesson and hands on learning. Christine insists we stop at the candy store and at least let her smell the yummy treats. We're making progress, learning life's lessons and content in our version of "normal."

Chateau Lake Louise is a beautiful lakeside hotel but overrun with tourists, including girls that capture the boys' interest. Everyone, except for Michael and Jeff rent canoes on the pristine alpine carved lake. The boys think it's a stupid idea and go off in search of cute girls. The scenery from the canoe is inspiring and the serenity of the lake powerful from the canoe. The bluish glacier that carved this lake humbly rests on the summit and ever so slowly creeps along, alive and showing it still possesses the clout to move mountains. The turquoise blue lake is crystal clear with white caps from the brisk wind; the bright orange canoes seem suspended, tethered by an unseen hand.

In my canoe, I enjoy a serious "deja-vu" as thirty years ago Tracy and I were canoeing on this very same lake together as teenagers. Now, as adults we are with our own teenaged girls in the same spot reliving a cherished childhood moment. This is a true testament to our parents, who so devoted themselves to teaching us a love of travel, nurturing our adventurous spirits and the colossal power of family.

The Burberry clad tourists with expensive, high-tech cameras on the hiking trails of Lake Louise are an interesting sight. Afraid to get their perfect outfits stained and dirty or too much sun, they are clearly exposed to elements they are not accustomed to. Wanting the photo opportunity of the fleeting moment only, seeming to miss the experience the trail speaks. I see myself in this lesson from the trail, the superficial life I masked my pain in, pain from life, un-charted and unexpected. The mask I wore . . . accomplished, seemingly together even through crisis, the self I presented to the world, picture perfect or so it seemed. Learning that on this road I travel, life is messy, and only by shedding my mask can it truly be appreciated for the glorious gift it is!

Our first cookout on a rickety old grill at our cabins and we are ravenous! We gorge on chicken, buffalo burgers, hot dogs, salad, French fries and ice cream. The picnic table is covered with a plastic red checkerboard tablecloth with an ant motif. The red wine is uncorked, and we're drinking Merlot from plastic cups. Content without the niceties that adorn the finest venues, we have abandoned the perfection and orchestration we had been accustomed to and now indulge in the joy of simplicity. Laughter and talking, all at once, we are exhilarated by our memorable cookout. Ashley dances at the grill, guards come down, all the children now dancing like buffalo without shame, with joy and security that family is everything and the only thing we truly have of value. My yardstick of success permanently changed, measuring life by experiences, moments and people, not things. It was never about "things," how had I believed that brazen lie?

Bad news creeps in, breaking news as London is brutally attacked by terrorists who bombed subways and tourist buses. It is England's own 9–11 with many injured and lost. Fear is on our minds as we wait to see if another shoe drops and more vicious attacks occur. We are in Canada, gone from the perceived security that home offers. Aloud I wonder what our border return to the United States will be like. We pray together for those affected, for all of us in this troubling moment. Tracy, Bruce, Ashley and I leave for a night hike. I must draw away from the television, sucking me in its web. The immediacy of news is hypnotic and unhealthy. I am falling under its spell. Michael, deeply sensitive, goes outside to throw a football around with Jeff. He feels fearful, unnerved, un-steadied and full of pain for the suffering souls in England.

First stop on the night hike, Moraine Lake, an iridescent color blue surrounded by Ten Peaks. Yes, we really count ten named peaks. The lake is stunning to see and offers a relaxing hike. Colorful canoes rest against the emerald and sapphire backdrop waiting. We see a Canadian warning sign, in English and French to travel in groups of six to avoid confrontations with bears. Can bears count? Will they know we are only four? We debate these questions as though this is our only care in the world. We travel Bow Valley Parkway for wildlife sightings but only one large elk appears with a big rack. Onto Johnston Canyon Falls, a narrow slot canyon that you follow a catwalk to traverse. An exciting climb made all the more interesting by perching on the edge of the canyon wall, suspended hundreds of feet above the raging cascade, the spray chilling us to the bone in the cool night air. The falls gather locomotive momentum before plunging into the towering rock walls they have aptly carved these thousands of years. Again, I am humbled by time, by life and by natural forces stronger than us all. Fireflies appear and chase us home to our little log cabins near the lake.

It is 10:30 and light outside. Michael and Jeff are still throwing a football, the TV silenced. It seems too light outside to sleep so we're restless. Or is it the news from London? Finally, at midnight it is dark although not pitch dark. We are tucked in, a family of five, our larger family of nine, in the vast Canadian woods thankful to be together.

25

SAFARI NIGHT

A beautiful Canadian morning! Eh? Sunny, crisp, cool mountain air and clear blue skies take my breath away. Still, not Crater Lake Blue though. Will the color blue always be judged by Crater Lake? Bacon and egg breakfast cooked on an antique cast iron skillet readies our day and is enjoyed al fresco on our deck overlooking the lush green forest and Lake Louise Ski Area. Everyone eats to their fill and we are off. The caravan presses on to Takakkaw Falls, a stunning, icy and dangerous 1,000 foot falls. The terrain defies gravity, switchbacks, steep slopes with crumbling rocks and formidable heights. The narrow trail struggles to maintain boundaries between human and natural forces, so necessary for the survival of both. It is a challenging hike pushing our limits to extremes, showing me once again we are capable of more than we believe ourselves to be.

Emerald Lake in Yoho National Park, British Columbia reminds me of a trip to Ireland. The color green is vibrant with life. Surrounded by mountains on all sides, the lake is beauty and colors unspoiled. The many shades of green and abundant wild flowers, burn under the face of a glacier that was carved since the beginning of time. The Lake appears reflective and bares all I hold inside. The mirrored reflection speaks out loud, screaming to be heard and to know it will be remembered long after I leave.

Another natural wonder, "Oh goodie," Ashley replies, the mountains, waterfalls and scenic beauty all blending together. She's seen one mountain she's seen them all. I assure her that in her own time, she will come to appreciate this glorious creation and gain perspective about this extreme family journey. She sulks, returning to the car for her own introspective hike, pushing away.

What will she remember later, a miserable family vacation or the absolute knowledge of her place in my heart? Knowing I cannot control what she remembers, it is OK to let go of the expectation of perfection in family life and realize we are what we are, patina and all. Perfection is overrated anyway! I am embracing imperfections and ridding myself of the intense need to please everyone all the time. Lose the mirages life sets up as real. Of all lessons for my children to remember, this is most important. It's also the one I have the most control over since by releasing my excessive expectations of them and myself, we are freed to be who we're truly meant to be. The reflections of my heart bared, revealed to me by the lake, screaming to be heard and crying to be remembered when we return home. Perhaps ADD and LD are really imperfection at their finest! Won't the mean girls be astonished to learn that!

Dinner on the "Barbie" as our cabin housekeeper calls it. Delicious and we are again ravenous after the strenuous wilderness hikes at the falls and lake. Everything tastes better in the fresh, crisp mountain air. We're inspired from our hiking adventures and are sharing highlights of the trails over dinner.

Our evening visit to Banff, a chic little mountain town provides fun for all, including the men! Lovely wide boulevards with a French feel are adorned with overstuffed hanging flower baskets around the street lights. Banff is filled with restaurants (elk or buffalo chops anyone?), furriers, Indian boutiques and tee shirt shops, a patchwork of reckless merriment. It feels good to walk the streets and people watch, aimlessly, without purpose or expectation.

Expectations, always high expectations, self-imposed, society-imposed, it really doesn't matter. Being a prisoner to high expectations is a formidable and imposing wall. Losing these expectations gives me a wobbly feeling at first, an unknown course. I have been driven and guided by high expectations, a course I also put my children on. They chafe at the rigidity imposed on their wills, like I did. A realization that nearly knocks me over, is this I am doing to my own children? What I so desperately run from, what I am running from now, having expectations hoisted on me, driven to succeed even at great personal cost. I feel as though I've been struck by lightening with an intense penetration of thought raging through me—like the controlled burn of a forest fire consuming the debris of shattered expectations and clearing the way for new roots.

Returning from Banff, nine people in the Chief, having ditched the wagon train, we travel off road for Safari Night Two. In Jackson, Wyoming last summer a highlight evening was safari night to search for wildlife in the Grand Teton National Park. Tonight, we seek the same re-creation of carefree fun in a crammed and worn Chevrolet Suburban. Our expedition begins! With eighteen eager eyes, we search the dense forests for wildlife, having invaded the animal's diverse habitat in our large SUV. We see a free roaming herd of elk, more than thirty, including many babies who still wear their white spots. The mother elk call their dawdling baby elk to task. Does every mother do this? We spot three male elk with the largest racks we've ever seen and there's loud male boasting at this sight! Christine is in the back seat perfecting her elk call with encouragement all around and Ashley is out the sunroof with binoculars as though on African Safari.

Finally, Michael spots an enormous black bear he immediately nicknames Elvis. After three weeks of searching high and low through every national park we traversed, he is elated to find an American Black Bear, in Canada no less! Michael is the happiest I have seen him this trip . . . animals are his thing! Uncomplicated and non-judgmental, animals rock in Michael's world especially with the long awaited sighting of Elvis. One more grizzly bear in the distance, more elk and mule deer, so safari night is a huge success but, still no moose sighting . . . the ever elusive naughty moose. A frequent refrain can be heard, "Is it elk or moose? Oh, only elk!"

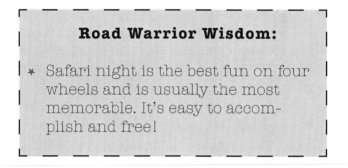

Road Warrior Wisdom:

* Safari night is the best fun on four wheels and is usually the most memorable. It's easy to accomplish and free!

Pig out night back at the cabins, ice cream eaten right out of the container, toast, buttered toast, popcorn (with ketchup) and leftovers, all eaten cold. The food doesn't matter; we laugh just watching ourselves, nine people in a cabin built for four gorging ourselves silly. We finish all our food because tomorrow we return to the United States. I awake in the middle of the night searching for stars in the Canadian sky but since the sky never gets truly dark this time of year there were few to be seen. A dim grey twilight is what the night sky shines.

As we pack our cabin, I contemplate again, twice in two years I am within driving distance to Alaska. I aspire to drive the Alaska Highway in my suburban with the dazzling landscape unfolding on the lone highway to the last American frontier. I wish we could go on yet we are feeling the time on the road. All but me are anxious to be heading east toward home; they are wearier than I anticipated at this juncture of the journey. Unsure whether the pace of travel, excessive sights, unpredictability of days or group dynamics, it is difficult to pinpoint the cause of our fatigue. This trip is bringing out the best and worst in each of us.

Perhaps the burning forest fires are a personal cleansing and renewal essential for future growth individually and as a family. Letting go of the expectations, spoken and unspoken and allowing each other the blessed joy of being themselves, without condemnation or judgment. ADD's greatest hope!

It's a tiring morning for us all as we return to the United States; travel keeps us on a very busy schedule. I pray that we have grown and bonded in new ways, ways that are not yet clear to us. I sympathize with Ashley, lumped in with the children and on the cusp of adulthood. Michael being away from home so long is unsteady with daily unpredictability, yet he remains in high spirits, struggling to adapt. Perhaps with a longer lens they will realize how much more we have in common than that which separates us. Has my personal quest for self realization amidst disorders asked too much of my family? Have I put us on a course of no return or are we charting a new one? Are we collapsing under the weight of miles, isolation and unpredictability or do we just need a rest? The forest fires rage and consume everything in its path. I leave my Alaskan dreams behind, again thinking, some day . . . one day.

26

LIFE IS MESSY!

Returning to the United States through immigration is surprisingly simple given the chaos in London. A few questions, our passports are in order and an orange from breakfast is confiscated since its country of origin is unknown. Welcome to Montana, a new state. Rest stop in Babb, another town for the unusual names book and on into Glacier National Park, our fourteenth national park this trip.

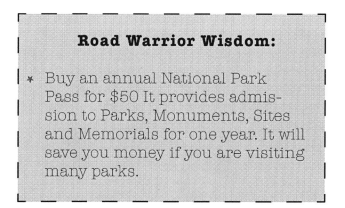

Road Warrior Wisdom:

* Buy an annual National Park Pass for $50 It provides admission to Parks, Monuments, Sites and Memorials for one year. It will save you money if you are visiting many parks.

Immediately upon entering the Park, a bear traffic jam! It's a National Park phenomenon that occurs frequently during wildlife sightings. There are abandoned cars, some still running with car doors open, as spectators run to see a tiny little bear cub grazing the meadow. Christine is now out the sunroof, not to be outdone by her brave big sister. Kodak moments as cameras click at a rapid rate, with everything the small cub does saved on film to show the world we are the adventurous breed we claim to be.

We arrive at Many Glacier Hotel, and another check in *Great Lodges of the National Parks*. We're welcomed by a trio of shaggy mountain goats, frolicking in the parking lot. They're accustomed to human invasion and continue to graze without a care in the world. The Swiss chalet styled hotel has beautiful hand carved woodwork and a massive copper fireplace gracing the enormous three story lobby. The fireplace resembles a campfire and is a communal spot for visitors eager to share their personal adventure stories, best hikes and wildlife sightings. The shrinking bluish glaciers are visible from the floor to ceiling paned window testifying to time itself; ebbing, flowing, retreating and changing.

Ashley beams, finding an ancient coin operated pay telephone in an old wooden booth since her cell service has vanished. Christine and I search for huckleberry ice cream, a regional delicacy and Michael goes hiking along Swiftcurrent Trail. Alone, and at peace, to explore a world that suits him, wide-open and untamed, with me hoping he discovers the best buried treasure of all, his wonderful, spirited and courageous self. Finding dreams can still be dreamt in this open land he loves.

Tracy and I share a nostalgic moment. We stayed at Many Glacier nearly thirty years ago with our parents, and so we try to stay in the same rooms but they're booked solid. Yes, as overly organized teenagers we kept a log of every room number and expense on our trips west—OCD apparently with me long before it had a name! Tracy and I find the rooms we stayed in, for posterity. The rooms are the smallest in the hotel facing the parking lot without the coveted Swiftcurrent Lake view or immense balcony. The housekeeper just happens to be cleaning so we sneak a glimpse into our past. A light goes on in my heart, realizing immediately, the extraordinary sacrifices my parents made to give their daughters' lifelong experiences honed by travel, wanderlust and togetherness with an absolute knowledge of their unconditional love. They did not travel the country without us; it certainly would have been easier, surely more restful. Instead, they took us on the adventure of their lifetime understanding life lessons from the trips might not be remembered or appreciated until much later in life, sacrificing where they stayed to accommodate for six rather than the luxury of a table for two. Will my own children recognize this precious gift? Lessons the multitudes of miles reveal.

Good old-fashioned comfort food. After eating regionally for three weeks, we gorge on pizza and pasta at a local Italian restaurant. Pepperoni pizzas are devoured and pasta bowls licked clean. Laughter fills the table with everyone talking at once competing to tell the best story. What comfort food does best, it lets our guards down and brings familiarity and solace.

No television at Many Glacier Hotel, we're delivered from the electronic monster. The cousins, even Michael and Jeff play Candyland and charades for hours. Meaningful childhood moments come from foolhardy fun and our evening is filled with this amusement. The cousins are fortunate to share this time together developing long-lasting friendships that hopefully will transcend their parents. A legacy I aspire to leave, like footprints on a trail.

We are off on an early morning three mile hike, awakening our spirits on the Swiftcurrent Trail, circling the lake. This is for adults only, providing the teenagers an opportunity to sleep in. We are ready for a little elbow room having traveled and lived in close quarters with our children twenty-four hours a day, for days on end.

Swiftcurrent Lake is crystal clear though not as blue as Crater Lake, again the color blue is judged harshly. I wish I could bottle the pine scented woodsy smell, and take it home as my aromatherapy, returning me to this magical moment. Wild flowers in rainbow hues are reflected in the meditative lake. The face of the glacier too, appears in the depths of the lake's gaze, a picturesque calendar comes to life before my eyes.

Tracy and I see signs warning of bear and instantly are on the lookout through the dense woods, like veteran explorers. We want to see a bear, just not up close on this trail! Kevin announces he has "a Leatherman tool so no need to fear!" Like Father, like son, and, as with the Zippo . . . I think I'll take my chances. We quicken our pace, our eyes wide and intent. It's a grand hike around the trail and we're refreshed and ready to return to civilized society.

The serenity felt from the long hike is fleeting as we return to find civilized society is another mirage and learning that chaos has erupted back at the rooms. We thought we did our children a favor by letting them sleep in when we quietly left for our morning hike. Unfortunately, while we were out they woke and went wild. Confinement, boredom or teenage hormones, the trigger is hard to pinpoint but we are not happy and the hotel management is even unhappier! The paper thin walls reveal every word to other guests and cousins are pointing fingers for blame. It is easy to look accusingly at the ADD child first for this mayhem since so often that's where it seems to start. But I am reminded by the road to rewind the tape we usually play and calmly resolve the tensions run amuck. Ignoring my clenched fist and sore jaw, a reflex from this sudden stress as we get to the bottom of the chaos, begun simply by bored and confined teenagers! Lifelong friendship, perhaps we must think smaller at this point, friends for today. Forgiveness comes quickly between the cousins and from us as well, road warrior travel can bring out the best and worst in us all and we cannot press on mad at each other. Hugs, handshakes and apologies . . . life goes on. Perhaps this is how their bonds of friendship grow, weathering the storms of life.

At the almost famous Park Café in St. Mary's, a Glacier gateway town, we indulge in a tasty brunch, al fresco. Their motto is "Pie for Strength" and they have won me over on that slogan alone. When Christine orders her brunch the waitress asks if she wants a child's menu, her reply is, "Since I do not know when my next meal is, I better order an adult portion now!"

Mealtime on our adventure is unpredictable since food seems secondary to the frantic pace of miles, sights and moments. Food, even unimportant wanting only what is absolutely necessary for the energy to press on. The most meaningful and memorable meals come in unexpected moments—rattlesnake appetizers in Texas, campfire dinners with buffalo burgers and gooey S'mores, picnics at the falls on an old blanket and Mexican food mountainside in Weed. The simple things!

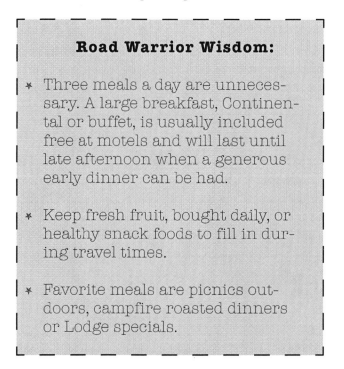

Road Warrior Wisdom:

* Three meals a day are unnecessary. A large breakfast, Continental or buffet, is usually included free at motels and will last until late afternoon when a generous early dinner can be had.

* Keep fresh fruit, bought daily, or healthy snack foods to fill in during travel times.

* Favorite meals are picnics outdoors, campfire roasted dinners or Lodge specials.

The Road to the Sun drive allows us to drink in the extraordinary beauty of Glacier as we traverse twenty-two miles along a steep narrow cliff hugging road while winding through the park to West Glacier. Sharp, jagged mountain peaks tower over us and white water streams slither through hills. Bluish glacier ice creeps slowly, alive and with purpose. The Stanley Glacier is receding at an alarming rate, no longer the majestic being it once was. We wonder aloud what Glacier National Park will be called if the glaciers are gone in time and debate whether this is caused by global warming. Logan Pass marks the Continental Divide. Weeping Wall cries to be seen. I am touched even after one month on the road by such surpassing grandeur.

Bear sighting ahead, in fact two bears. An American Black Bear who is actually brown and an enormous Grizzly Bear perched on an outcropped rocky ledge majestically keeping watch over his Park domain. It's clear he knows he's the star of the show! Bear traffic jam as they both attract quite an audience. Michael is running down the open road for a better glimpse with his binoculars and video camera on full duty as I relish the sight.

Big Horn Sheep are living symbols of the wilds of Glacier. They precariously cling to the mountains by a thread, perfectly balanced and crisscrossing the steep terrain. Mountain goats also call Glacier home. A large mountain goat at the edge of the roadway seems posed for the cameras. A herd of hillside goats with their babies, clinging to a craggy, steep slope, are fleeing the Red Jammer buses and hoards of people seeking solitude.

Red Jammer tour buses are a national park tradition. Begun with the automotive age, with open rollback canvas tops they have entertained tourists since the 1930's. They were recently refurbished to provide nostalgic park tours. Loaded with camera totting tourists the Jammers are a frequent sight in the heart of Western national parks.

Unsurpassed grandeur dominates the landscape as mountains soar to majestic heights. The Road to the Sun is exquisite. Now appreciated with my blinders removed, allowing me to discover the most precious and unique things in life cannot be built by hand or bought with currency, instead it's the simple, beautiful and random moments that we hold so dear. The gift of God's magnificent creation unwrapped.

Lake McDonald Lodge is our favorite National Park Lodge of the trip, defined by charming rustic elegance and Swiss styled influence. Formerly a hunting lodge, there are stuffed animal species very familiar to our drive today adorning the walls. An uncommon sight in the national parks to see the wildlife stuffed! The salmon colored lobby walls glow and the hand painted parchment lanterns add a friendly touch. The massive stone fireplace was once the kitchen fireplace and warms us with its crackling refrain.

Our last day as nine! We rush to squeeze in the final adventures and fleeting memories, not wanting to miss anything, eager to make more memories. What will be remembered has a new urgency. Now after millions of single seconds I recognize, that it is not the "things" but the moments and people that are the truest treasures in my life, and the memories are what I will take home as souvenirs.

Trinket mementos will gather dust, photographs will fade with time and even rocks can crumble to nothing, a beautiful lesson I learned from a fiery red rock that called to me from the hot Nevada desert last summer. I carried it home for 3,000 miles and put it near my front door to remind me of precious and fleeting seconds, of being in the moment of time where you are, cherishing life itself as the gift it is and remaining steadfast in the face of turmoil. But, the rock was not meant to live outside its desert home. In the harsh eastern climate with snow, wind, rain and ice it disintegrated before my eyes, teaching me a far more valuable lesson. Things do not last, even rocks. We must live within our own elements and not someone else's in order to bear our full beauty and potential, to be all we are created to be. What is lasting and true is my faith in God, the legacy of love I leave to those around me and simple joy filled moments with the people I cherish.

The cousins, minus Ashley, who chooses the adult path, are

frolicking in the frigid glacial Lake McDonald. Squeals of joy radiate from the children echoing down the wide open lake. A small antique boat passes by with passengers bundled up like they are in the Alaskan tundra. They are taking pictures of the crazy kids swimming in the frigid lake waters. The wonder and simplicity of childhood is before my eyes. True unabashed delight shines in their faces. Undaunted, even unaware of people's expectations or judgments, they are fascinated by the rocks, big and small, shapes and colors. Finding the Grinch shaped rock as they dive like veteran explorers for buried treasure. These uncomplicated and rapturous moments are where true memories are made.

We enjoy dinner al fresco, on the porch of our tiny cabin. It is only turkey sandwiches, but they taste like the finest gourmet food. The plastic ant covered checkerboard tablecloth is recycled for this, our last feast together. Razzleberry pie, a blueberry, raspberry and blackberry pie from Park Café tops off our feast, eaten with spoons right out of the tin. Our mouths stained purple by the colorful berries. Messy, like life! This is a meal to be remembered, not for the food, but for the fellowship, the place and the rich shared time together. We are blessed.

Ceremonial activities begin in earnest as we digest the pie. Walking stick medallions from the many national parks are affixed to Michael and Jeff's hiking sticks for bragging rights and perhaps their own sons one day. A bumper sticker ceremony ensues for the Chief as we affix a version of a medallion on the Suburban documenting its own well-worn travel. Time for favorites; favorite national parks, favorite lodges, favorite experiences, even favorite meals attest to our journey as nine. Special shared memories of a life well lived, our manifesto, of sorts!

Sleepy time in the Montana woods under the ever watchful Big Sky, moonlight dancing on the lake. No one wants this night to end, least of all me. The east is calling me home. Am I ready?

I see Michael sleeping soundly in the next bed and notice

a tiny tuft of grey in the front of his shaggy tousled hair. From little boy to young man he looks exactly like his father when we first met twenty-two years ago. Tears come to my eyes as though this is a sign I'm meant to see, telling me that everything will be OK after all.

27

Moving Shadow over Mountains

One more activity before we leave spectacular Lake McDonald, horseback riding at the Mule Shoe Outfitters inside the park. A trail ride traveling on horseback to explore the far reaches of Glacier and Wild America. The wanna be cowboys and lone cowgirl Christine are saddled and ready for their sight-seeing adventure. The mangy horses are in line formation, head to tail, instinctively following the horse ahead in perfect compliance. Why does this feel like a metaphor for my past life, society's expectations for Michael and me, plodding along mundane, masked and un-spirited?

The two-hour trail ride goes hopelessly awry when the cowboy guide leading the charge gets lost in the deep Montana woods that suddenly appear the same wherever they turn. Three hours lost on a rocky, steep and windy trail. Bruce rides without stirrups, prepared to jump if necessary while Christine's horse nearly throws her, rearing up on his hind legs, when spooked by a narrow bridge crossing. It is *Survivor* lived out in the Montana Mountains. Relieved to dismount and shower the trail smells away, the honorary cowboys and cowgirl proudly recount their near misses and amazing survival throughout the unforeseen escapade.

It is hard to leave the peaceful and slow pace of Lake

McDonald, a respite for our souls. Solitude and refuge are found here and I am reluctant to leave, knowing what waits. The mountains are a watchtower over me. Forces that shaped this landscape are shaping and altering Michael and me as well. Change is a slow process not an event, but I can feel and see in Michael the past eroding away with miles and fires burning deeply, no longer meandering to life's expectations, and instead being ever mindful of moments, singular and unique. We have grown taking new and stronger roots, like wild flowers in the nourishing rain.

The caravan is eastbound, with Ashley leaving us in the other car, push-pull continues. It is a melancholy time sending her off on her own, without us. She will travel with her cousins as they fly east first thing tomorrow returning to jobs and lives with renewed spirits and western daydreams. We are all stronger from the endless miles traveled.

One more trading post, last minute treasures for friends at home brings a surprise meeting. An old craggy man behind the counter with telling haunts blue eyes intrigues us, eyes older than his years. We learn Owl, his Native American name, is an honorary adopted member of the Lakota Sioux Tribe. He has lived in a teepee and followed Native American customs since his twenties when he felt called to their way of life. Owl's sole lifelong ambition is to further the understanding of Native American and tribal customs. He founded the *Red Buffalo Society* to ensure this preservation and education of culture for others. It is astonishing meeting Owl.

Michael and I learn a lot from him about following our heart's great desire and living the life we know deep down we are meant to live. Even if that life does not meet the standards of certain social circles, a teepee for Owl is home. How futile it is to be someone other than who you are meant to be. Michael's differences, un-harnessed spirit and heightened sensitivity to the world around him now viewed as the great treasures they are. Too many people in society conform to someone else's expectations for them, instead of embracing the uniqueness that is theirs alone. ADD, a fragile and precious gift, shaping Michael distinctively. The wisdom of Owl's words echo loudly. I know we are meant to hear what he has shared. Ashley purchases a necklace of antique Indian trading beads, some over 400 years old, with a *Red Buffalo Society* medallion that belongs to Owl attached. One souvenir I am very glad she returns with.

We follow as a caravan for the final eighty seven miles of our 2,500 shared miles together. Radio contact continues until the concluding bittersweet goodbye. Tearful goodbyes at Elmo, on Flathead Lake inside Flathead Indian Reservation, as our road together parts. Ashley and her cousins travel west to the airport and Kevin, Michael, Christine and I, east, final destination, Home Sweet Home, no matter the course. We all talk at once! Goodbyes, love you, hugs, safe travel and the perennial question, when and where is our next adventure. Greece passes our lips. It is sad to see them go and for the next ten miles I am quiet, absorbed in my own thoughts, with the melancholy that comes with the end of something special.

For our eastbound travel, Kevin joins us! I am unnecessarily nervous at how we will all fair, one more person and personality in the car, confined with 3,000 miles to traverse. Will we survive each other? Michael, who is accustomed to being the "man" of the car now seems excited to share the ropes of long distance travel with his dad. Michael and Christine seated next to each other with little personal space? I pray for peace.

The big sky claim in Montana is well deserved and we feel minuscule under its immensity. Brilliant white puffy clouds with rainbow colors peeking from the fringe hover over the land feeling close enough to touch. Kevin notices the shadows of the clouds moving across the mountains and is instantly inspired to make that my Native American name, "Moving Shadow over Mountains." I love it and it fits me perfectly, not caring a bit what others might think of this carefree road warrior nonsense.

Kevin prefers the dusty scenic two-lane road less traveled

and says he "can travel like this eastbound." Unfortunately, with 2,000 miles to go to his brother's house in Illinois and four days to travel, we need an interstate highway! Interstate 90 East it is, crossing Montana. Not a typical interstate as we are pleased and surprised to see. The roadway offers a spectacular climb through rugged snow capped mountains, crisscrossing rivers and sandstone monoliths all as the Big Sky towers like a canopy above us. There are very few cars and trucks on the wide paved road so Kevin gets a taste of the pleasure I feel driving in the west.

Michael and Christine settle quickly into life as four on the road. It is more confining in the car on the return trip so they must now share a bench seat. We scrounge through the packed full car for the long lost fun bags, now buried deep. The no DVD rule has fallen, so *Shrek 2* will entertain. Why not, I rationalize; they have already seen more this past month than many people see in a lifetime. I ease up and let go of my rigid expectations. The shared pillow between them with their heads touching at the crowns testament enough to what they have learned on the road we've traveled.

We pass Three Forks where Lewis and Clark came to three forks in the Missouri River. They named the rivers, Jefferson, Gallatin and Madison. We cross the Madison and Gallatin Rivers. Lewis and Clark took the Jefferson River, the southwestern fork on their bold journey west. There are markers all along Interstate 90 with the Lewis and Clark trail head, symbolic that we are on terrain that Lewis and/or Clark traversed two hundred years ago on their historic journey. I am humbled and awed by their feat over this treacherous terrain. On foot and in keel boats they traveled westward in search of adventure and answers.

Christine asks if we're stopping in Butt, Montana not realizing it is called Butte. Michael is instantly inspired to add Butte to his list. The miles quickly pass. The sun is setting behind us, a strange feeling as we are no longer chasing the setting western sun, but it seems to be chasing us away. I photograph the shadow of our car as we drive through the red and yellow sunset landscape. Michael and Christine are singing off key, "Home, Home on the Range," memorable Road Warrior moments we share. The stars reflect off the mountains like shimmering jewels. Stars so bright they shine to the horizon. No moon tonight so the coyote are quiet. A cacophony of crickets bid us good night.

28

LETTING GO

At last, a two room family suite where we are no longer stumbling over each other in a tiny cramped motel room, it's heavenly! For the first time throughout the entire trip, Kevin and I have a room to ourselves. We tuck the children in and retreat to our own room for uninterrupted conversation, solitude and peace. Time alone to reconnect, my lost soul crying out to be heard, held and understood. The fires blazed through me over the many miles, I am found, freed and prepared to return to our life at home. Forever changed by the lessons on the road.

Kevin wakes me at ten; I am physically exhausted and emotionally spent and needed a good night's sleep. He surprises me with Montana made, heart-shaped silver earrings with stars to remind me always that he understands, respects and loves the real me. Seeing my wanderlust for the gift it is, our shared and individual dreams are once again rekindled.

We check e-mails to make re-entry easier and finally eat brunch at noon, six hours past our normal daily westbound departure time. Michael looks at me with incredulous eyes at our relaxed, random departure time. As though he knows this was the real pace we were meant to find all along. Life lived on life's term and not orchestrated by forever high expectations and rigid schedules. My expectations and life's expectations in this age of acceleration; our bodies and souls never designed to go so fast, the nanosecond pace society drives. He is comfortable with the tempo we've found, more to his natural rhythm and need. A relaxed smile crosses his handsome face and I glimpse the dimple on his cheek, exactly like his father's. The stress fractures there a month ago have melted away in the summer sun. Hope courses through me like cool water extinguishing a blaze.

I too, love the pace of travel we have found. A new rhythm of the road that feels leisurely, more lighthearted and fun. Is this perspective the changes the road wrought? I now recognize safety and logistical challenges of our journey westbound, a mother alone with two children for long days and miles. I am glad to have taken the road I did, alone, it gives me the fresh perspective that I now hold. I also know I would drive west alone again in a heartbeat . . . the wilds of Alaska still call to me. Road Warrior life, my respite!

Our first leg stretch stop is Pompey's Pillar, a National Historic Landmark east of Billings. On the large sandstone monolith is "W. Clark July 25, 1806," the only known signature of Lewis or Clark on the famous Lewis and Clark Trail. I have chills seeing Clark's signature and recognize that I am standing in his steps. My spirit hears the brave adventurer's call and wanderlust inherent in all who travel to this sacred spot. Clark, leaving the banks of the Yellowstone River (Lewis and Clark called it the Elk River) left his mark to inspire future wanderers to share in his spirited nature and great sense of adventure. Sacagawea, her baby Pomp, who the rock is named for and York, Clark's devoted African slave, stood here too, having journeyed to the Pacific Ocean and back with Clark, sharing the exotic wonders.

We meet an interesting Crow Tribe Native American guide who is related to the original owner of the pillared rock. He is well-built from years in the mountains and it's impossible to read his age on his sun worn face. He wears denim Wrangler jeans, a long sleeved shirt with pearl snap buttons and snakeskin cowboy boots even in the hot dry summer heat. The Guide is fluent in the Crow Tribe language and also Native American sign language that he worries is a dying art. He, like Owl, is on a mission to bring well-deserved respect to Native Americans both within the tribes and outside to non-Native Americans. I ask for a photograph to remember him by, seeing and appreciating the collision of cultures, lifestyle choices and expectations. Reminding Michael of H. Jackson Brown Jr.'s remark, "People take different roads seeking fulfillment and happiness. Just because they're not on your road doesn't mean they've gotten lost." It fits my own ADD son and me to a tee.

A rest stop in Terry, Montana and yes, it makes Michael's list. Terry is a sleepy little country town with one traffic light, a pawnshop and abandoned storefronts. We drink a refreshing cold pop, soda to easterners, and buy a Terry coffee mug at a gift shop. The townspeople are very friendly and offer local sightseeing advice but we must push on.

Ashley calls and is home, safe and sound. She is happy and relieved to see flat, civilized land again, yet misses us, push-pull. She is in that glorious time of life when friendships seem forever and life is filled with unlimited potential. Insight I am sometimes slow to see yet can still hold true for me.

Hello North Dakota, a new state.

North Dakota surprises with its beautiful Badlands. Visiting the Theodore Roosevelt National Park in Medora, we see harsh and forbidding ranges with beautiful multi-colored hills and prickly sagebrush. President Roosevelt deserves significant credit for the development of the National Park Service and the ultimate preservation of National Park treasures. He spent a great deal of time in these Badlands and grew to love this wild unbridled land. His tiny log cabin with one room and a fireplace for warmth still stands. Roosevelt National Park has typical Western animals but we are thrilled anyway to see a prairie dog town and two enormous bison, the trademark Western animal. It would not be an adventure without seeing bison graze in the open range. Last summer, we saw herds of bison in Wyoming and South Dakota and took their abundance for granted; Michael remembers his bison from Yellowstone National Park. He stood within two feet of this strong, unpredictable animal and yet was unafraid, at peace alongside the giant beast, sensing a kindred spirit.

Crossing the Missouri River, the same river Lewis and Clark navigated west, is exciting, especially after Michael's Lewis and Clark research prior to the trip. There are replica keel boats on the shore similar to the ones in Onewa, Iowa, marking the two hundredth anniversary of their journey west. I encourage Michael to remember the lesson's learned by their expedition: perseverance, tenacity, fortitude, resourcefulness and forward thinking. Life lessons for him, for me and for all ADD children. I tell Michael and Christine that I believe Lewis and/or Clark were ADD too, how else would they not have been daunted by their undertaking! Crossing the United States without the slightest idea of what they would encounter. Rumors in the East mentioned wooly mammoths, glaciers and unknown natives. Lewis and Clark and ADD Children, fearless spirited souls. ADD certainly has its benefits.

Road Warrior Wisdom:

* Read up on sites before you travel!

We cross into Central Time and it is still light outside at ten, the sun just setting. Michael screams "hurricano" and is punchy from the long hours driving today, a sign it is time to get off the road. Jamestown, North Dakota it is. We are back to our motel venue, real life on life's terms.

At 2:00 a.m., my cell phone jars me out of a sound sleep.

Every mother's worst nightmare is flashing through my mind… car accident. Flooded with emotion and adrenaline, my heart is racing. I am relieved to hear Ashley's small voice, sighing on the phone telling me she has a stomach ache and only needs her mother and the consolation that brings. Push-Pull as college looms. "I love you Mama," Ashley says as she hangs up her phone. "I love you more," I whisper back. A mother always loves more.

29

Faith, Hope and Pancake Breakfast

We enter Minnesota and stop at Fergus Falls for breakfast at a pancake house. We're ravenous, ordering grand slam platters and again clean our plates!

During breakfast, we're intrigued by an ancient gentleman with hollow cheeks; eyes magnified by thick glasses, sun worn furrows and wearing denim coveralls at least two sizes too big. We are fascinated by him, wondering his life story. Is his wife dead and gone? Friends, has he most likely outlived them all? All alone, he sits and eats with his frail opaque arm wrapped around his plate supporting himself upright. He only eats a small cup of soup and wraps the tiny half sandwich remaining in his used napkin.

"Is this his only meal of the day?" Michael queries, our captivation with him continuing. He puts a few small coins down on the table for a tip and shuffles to the cash register. Kevin, at the register in half the time, treats him to his meal saying he reminds him of his own long gone granddad. A random act of kindness on the long road of life and we are giddy with the experience. Christine insists we pray for him tonight!

Faith and hope are powerful forces in my ADD/LD ravaged world. The absolute belief that God is in control and although the ADD road is not easy, it is never a road I travel alone. Brought to my knees by disorders, I found peace there. Prayer binds our family together, supports me through long lonely stretches, releases me from expectations of control and assures me that I do not fight this battle alone. Worry and fear about an unknown future no longer necessary with a known God. Patience, hope, forgiveness and fortitude are so necessary on my path. Hope is the strongest weapon I have in the ADD battle.

We enjoy carefree fun at the Mall of America near Minneapolis and a necessary break after a full morning of interstate driving. It's the largest mall in the U.S. and has an amusement park, an aquarium and a chapel just in case you want to be married at the mall. Christine and I shop until I drop using her birthday gift cards to select a clean fresh summer outfit. Kevin and Michael enjoy indoor NASCAR simulated racing and are beaming after their respective races, breathlessly sharing every detail of their amazing race car experience. Michael and Christine beg to stay for movies, rides and restaurants but we must push on. Five hundred miles "back to Mahomet," Illinois to visit Kevin's brother. We must make a dent in those miles tonight.

Road Warrior Wisdom:

* Kid friendly venues are definitely worth stopping to see. They are carefree fun and a good change of pace from historical sights and National Parks. Mitchell Corn Palace, Graceland and a rodeo in Buffalo, Wyoming are favorites.

We cross the Mississippi River and I know the West is gone. We are officially east of the Mississippi, and there is no celebration this time. Reality waits on the fringe like a cold shower. Can

I flee, or is it too late? The ache and pull of the west is still strong within me, as real as anything I've ever known.

Wisconsin, America's Dairyland! The miles parade by green-pastured farms with pretty red barns, and sunflowers standing tall, like tin soldiers in perfect formation. It is 8:40 and the sun is setting. My pulse races with rapid thoughts and uneasiness about returning to a world I fear I hardly recognize after lessons from the west. Humidity creeps in like a heavy blanket and now I know I'm east. Our windshield is newly cracked and almost impossible to see through from splattered mosquitoes, we must stop the car twice to clean it. I shudder with a feeling of "get me out of here," surely I'm not ready to return to a land of named houses and whitewashed lives.

We stop early at Black River Falls, Wisconsin for a restful night's sleep. Hot showers, clean clothes and four sets of teeth are brushed twice for good measure; we want to look civilized for Kevin's brother tomorrow.

I pack away my hiking backpack, worn, dusty boots and relaxed western clothes with a heavy heart. I rummage through the car for my designer pocketbook that no longer seems to be my style. It looks like a foreign object I no longer recognize. I pull "normal" clothing from my suitcase to dress presentably for my brother-in-law's family. The clothing feels tight and confining like an outgrown pair of pants. My new found confidence from lessons of the West is shaky. Yet what I heard and learned, feels more powerful and real than anything in my life. How do I continue to embrace these changes and make them last, for all of us, as we reenter the atmosphere and routine of real life?

Real life marching on, waiting for no one as I learn a forty-two year old girlfriend, with teenagers, is pregnant with her third child and a fifty-two year old friend is dying of cancer with eighteen months or less to live. Life and death pressing on, time waits for no one. I ask once again, what will be important in my life ten years from now? What will be remembered? How will I now perceive time and events with my newfound lessons from the road and changed heart?

30

BACK TO MAHOMET

Our last night in a motel for this trip, do I mourn or celebrate? Will we adapt to a new home life or fall back into one of expectations? Life is no longer tied in a pretty little package nor, judged or lived as ordinary, but expanded and rich with new meaning. When will my wanderlust rear its head? Can ADD/LD define us in a new way, rejoicing in home life lived on ADD life's terms? Spontaneous, creative and imperfect! These thoughts roll gently through my heart as I pack for home.

Cheese, cranberries and hot cinnamon rolls for breakfast, we are clearly in the Midwest. Mahomet, Illinois here we come, back to Mahomet for a second visit, since last summer only Michael and I forged there. After our special visit then, we promised to return and now we honor that pledge with Kevin and Christine in tow, excited to see family.

Our final shopping of the trip in Normal, Illinois and as I'm navigating, Kevin asks, "How far is Normal?" How appropriate the name of this little town! Normal, being what I set off to find and returning from our road warrior odyssey, I now embrace the fact that no life is normal. That life itself is a gift and every journey is different and there is freedom in that understanding alone. I wonder why I had ever wanted normal anyway.

We select presents for Mark's birthday, flowers for Linda

and a few surprises for the cousins; we are anxious and ready for a great family visit. Michael offers me a flower, hand-picked from the parking lot, thanking me for the trip, his eyes darting shyly between me and the asphalt. I am taken back to Michael as a small boy presenting his handmade valentine heart to me. The crinkled red construction paper with the frayed and jagged edging adorned with white lace and uneven lettering spelling out his love for me. His eyes look exactly the same now, wide with devotion, this, a love note from his heart. Speaking the words he awkwardly wants said. Tears are streaming down my cheek as I wrap my arms around my now almost grown son, celebrating and cherishing "different." Content and abundantly blessed with our version of "normal."

We arrive in Mahomet, knowing my way to their home without directions. Mahomet is a charming train garden town, a perfect little slice of small town America. Corn and soybean fields surround Mahomet in a sweet cocoon as friendly neighbor's wave hello to every passing car. Isn't this the life I left a month ago? Now it appears wistful, serene and renewing . . . growing more than I imagined these last 9,000 miles.

Kevin is elated to see his youngest brother Mark; the two hug each other with might, realizing how much we needed this visit and how important it would be to Kevin to share this time here. Mark shakes his head in wonderment, amazed and surprised that Kevin is here. They are immediately inseparable with so much catching up to do. Linda is a perky petite brunette with bright round chestnut eyes, Midwest born and raised; she graciously welcomes our road weary family. Linda prepares a delicious Mexican dinner, enchiladas, beef (this is the Midwest!) tacos, corn tortilla chips, salsa made from her garden tomatoes and sweet corn pudding. A groaning board of delicious home cooked food that fills and nourishes us in a way we did not realize we needed, like Mahomet, like family. Michael gushes that this is his first home cooked meal in thirty days, asking for seconds and finally thirds. We eat to our fill, surrounded by the warmth and security of family that accepts us, imperfections and all, for whom and what we are.

The cousins, though shy and awkward at first, dive right into fun. They too become inseparable. Michael patiently warms up to his little cousin Allison and before long he is the galloping bronco with her piggyback like a "super hero" of the Wild West. She is thrilled and untamed; squealing with delight, to go faster, giddy up, like this is the ride of a lifetime. Michael is proud to be her hero. I see not only a carefree and relaxed smile on his face but his heart that's bigger than his chest. I beam just watching them. Michael heads off with his cousins, Matt and Jordan, who are accomplished musicians, for some serious guy time. After some powwowing they encourage Michael to try his hand on their electric guitar and drums. The "guys" are jamming and the house is rattling. Michael is having a blast, enthralled and energized by this new experience. The powerful beat of the drum and the pluck of the guitar string resonate with the life of ADD.

Christine is talking a mile a minute excitedly telling her wide-eyed cousins about our great adventures on the road. She is running outside, barefoot like a spirited wild child catching fireflies in an old glass jar. She includes blades of green grass in the bottom of the jar so the glowing fireflies "have something to eat tonight" and pokes holes in the metal lid so they "can breathe" as they shine for her, a twinkling and innocent bedside nightlight.

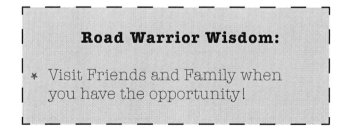

Road Warrior Wisdom:

* Visit Friends and Family when you have the opportunity!

31

Birthday Blessings

Happy birthday dear Mark, he turns forty-three today. An amazing "coincidence" that we could travel 9,000 miles and be in Mahomet on Mark's forty-third birthday? No, God engineered perfect timing.

Exhausted, I sleep until noon, thirteen hours of sound sleep like a bear in hibernation. Kevin startles me when he checks to see if I am breathing! The thousands of road warrior miles and days of trails have caught up with me; I am physically and emotionally spent. I need serious rest and Mark and Linda's home offers solace.

I wish Mark a happy birthday and hug him extra tight. Mark has battled Juvenile Diabetes, Type One since the age of eight. It's a vicious disease and puts tremendous strain on his whole body. Despite the physical strain and limitations, he heroically lives life to the fullest as Linda valiantly cares for and encourages him. Despite extreme edema in his legs that requires him to walk with a cane he is doing well and his prognosis appears promising. We celebrate today, this moment and Marks life, with the knowledge that none of life is forever, for any of us, and we recognize how blessed we are to be together. We are living in this moment clinging to it like a life raft knowing it's all that truly matters.

We visit the University of Illinois at Champaign/Urbana to see the National Center for Supercomputing, and marvel at Mark's life work. It's a fascinating cutting-edge high tech center with rooms of floor to ceiling computers glowing with life, calculating hypotheses to infinity. Corporate, academic and scientific research originates here under the watchful eye of genius, sheer genius. We enjoy Chicago style pizza for lunch at the college hangout, Papa Dell's. Thick crusted cheesy pepperoni pizza so rich I can only eat a single slice. Michael on the other hand eats three large slices and reaches for a fourth, a growing boy! Being the senior cousin, the first time this trip, he relishes the fact that the number of boys finally outweighs the girls. They huddle at their own end of the table . . . and he's the leader of the pack, holding court like a jester. Happy Birthday dear Mark is sung twice with restaurant patrons happily joining the refrain. Mark blushes deep crimson feeling true love from those around him celebrating with great joy.

Reality is closing in; the slow drive east is making the transition palatable. I don't know what waits for me at home; I only remember what I left. Will it be different? The tranquil mind set I return with and new knowledge of what matters most in my life will best ease the passage. I will plan ahead for our next adventure to Alaska, as we are within four states of completing our fifty states quest. Forward thinking, and not returning to the state of mind of what could have or should have been for this thinking is dangerous and debilitating, especially to one parenting children with special needs.

Linda prepares a scrumptious feast for Mark's birthday. Cowboy steaks grilled to mid-western perfection, salmon, Caesar salad and corn on the cob from a nearby farm. We top off dinner with Linda's famous coconut cake, singing happy birthday dear Mark once again with five sets of eager breaths "helping" blow out the candles. Linda's a marvelous professional baker and we're in heaven savoring the rich flavors.

We share a favorite family birthday tradition, a custom

invented in desperation. I say desperation because typically ADD brings a family to that, a feeling of absolute exasperation. No one was being kind to one another that long ago day or saying a single nice word. Everyone seemed mad, frustrated and angry, the tension rising by hurricane force. To end the bloodletting, I yelled "Stop! Enough! We are going to sit down at this table and everyone is going to say one nice thing they love about the others." It broke the cycle of anger raging in the children and welling up in me. The wall of pain and hurtful words dividing them came crashing down around them. They left the kitchen table relieved, loved and understood. Eventually this became our birthday tradition with everyone insisting the custom continues.

Tonight, we go around the table and each person will say what they love about the birthday person, Mark. It can be anything, sweet or funny. The only rule is it must be truly what you love about them. As we offer Mark words of affection, a radiant feeling surrounds us as we share what makes him special. This is a precious gift for all of us, not knowing when we will have time again, to speak and cherish these words of promise.

Last December, on Michael's birthday we shared the same tradition. It was serious and profound with Michael squirming at the breakfast table unaccustomed to hearing such positive things about himself. When we finished, "My turn," he exclaimed asking to share what he loved, about us. Still turning the tables and living life outside the box, just as the pre-school matron noticed so long ago. I hold his spoken words close to my heart and will remember them for the rest of my life. He looked at me, our eyes locked together and said, "You are the coolest Mom because you can drive eight hundred miles in a day and not break a sweat!" Lessons learned about the true meaning of life from my ADD son.

We are blessed in so many ways! Nourished physically, spiritually and emotionally with the love of family and cherishing the time we share together. Michael and Christine will miss their Mahomet cousins, whom they have grown close to. They are talking, jamming and playing late into the night trying to squeeze every minute of time together they can, well aware of our departure scheduled for early morning, and knowing this is their last huddle of the visit. It is with great joy I witness their budding friendship, transcending miles, time, differences and disorders.

Sweet dreams for all in Mahomet under quiet starry skies with a sliver of moon shining high. Fireflies twinkle like night lights in the clean country air and crickets hum a country tune.

32

FINAL DESTINATION...HOME

Homebound! Am I ready to get back in the Suburban? I instantly have a panicky feeling of being confined, as I climb back into the passenger seat and travel 800 miles home, the exact opposite feeling than when our journey began where the driver's seat was my ticket out and lifeline to freedom. Home now decisively calling to me.

A hearty Midwest breakfast, steak, eggs, biscuits, honey and fresh fruit! We are ready for a cattle drive or at least a drive to Maryland, home being our final destination today. Goodbyes and "so longs" are painful; cousins not wanting to be separated, ask "when can we see each other next," wanting to mark the calendar before we leave, to have something to look forward to. Rare, shared family time, and we bask in its warmth with the knowledge that the memories made together and friendship among cousins will last a lifetime. The legacy of giant Sequoias continues.

I ask Linda for a Mahomet bumper sticker for the Chief to mark that we were here. Leaving a part of ourselves behind in Mahomet, like a cairn marking the passage.

Route 74 eastbound, with our final descent into Maryland, where home fires burn. Canadian geese will soon arrive on the Shore with their proud V-formations and honking calls to signal fall is on its way. The road of great adventures will always call my name, but this journey is coming to a close. It is time to return to the real world. I return with a new perspective honed by miles and days on the road. Now, embracing the fun and enormous potential that life with ADD children brings and learning not to fight the disorder nor seeking conformity. Never knowing what the road has in store next, appreciating their intense sensitivity to the world around and openness to every experience life brings. Life lived on ADD life's own terms, for Road Warriors and moms with unique children. Forever forward, no more rear view mirror living for us, our old tapes burned in the forest fires of the road!

Indiana is flat and uninspiring, an "old state" as well. Intermittent rain, eastern drivers and crowded narrow highways slow our progress home. Stopped for gasoline, I am haunted by a woman I see at a convenience store. She has a swollen, ugly black eye, red tear stained cheeks, appearing to be in her thirties with stringy bleached hair and stooped posture as though life weighs her down. I want to help her, engage her, but I am frightened by the man she is with. He is stocky, wearing dirty clothes and unshaven with an angry scowl. His bloodshot eyes dart around in all directions like an animal protecting his turf. Is he the reason I wonder for her tears and bruised and blackened eye? He briefly leaves her in the car, alone, buying a six pack of cheap beer inside. Is this what feeds his fury, the alcohol, their circumstances? Why does she stay with him? Does she have no other choice? Does she feel confined by fate? She will not encounter my pleading glances and we drive away. I silently ask God to watch over her, to give her strength and remind her of choices, there are always choices.

We see fireworks for sale in Ohio, the neon colored store with the jumbo lettering screaming FUN. Michael desperately wants to stop for treasures to take home. We will not stop to buy Michael fireworks, so fireworks are what we get from him! His disappointment abruptly brings out the worst in him. He is suddenly agitated, angry and anxious. Anxiety, anger and ADHD, are a vicious cycle, never decisively knowing which triggers which, and usually sparked by a completely different emotion: embarrassment, loneliness, isolation, frustration or helplessness. Is he apprehensive about returning home, also, to expectations he remembers? Or frustrated at not getting his way? Or, does he even know? He seems far from me and impossible to reach, suffering in a terribly lonely wilderness.

I despair, my dreams dashed that I saved us by taking this 9,000 mile journey. Perhaps, salvation was too lofty a goal anyway, that's not mine to give. His growth instead, will come like the miles on the road, sometimes bumpy or smooth, long or short, dark and windy and sometimes even sunny and straight. One at a time without a singular moment that the light goes on and I know we're there, but instead an accumulation of experiences. A desert still lies between the disorders and healing, and crossing the desolate landscape is a painstakingly slow journey. One step at a time, without the quick fix I dreamed a mother could provide. I ache to my core at this profound reality.

He will cross this desert at his own pace, in his own way and in his own time. For then the changes and growth of the journey will be his and not mine, and his growth will be lasting, not temporary. Reaching deep inside and accepting who he finds, despite what society says, and recognizing the unique gifts he possesses. My seeing him this way alone is not enough.

Exhausted by the outburst, Michael sleeps in a deep, sound sleep, punctuated by restless primal groans. Kevin and I contemplate the episode, clueless once again to what incited the outburst and why it goes to extremes. Where are his shut off mechanisms? Michael consumes my thoughts for miles, my soul aches. I am melancholy and quiet, gazing out the rainy window, silently praying for guidance, tears stinging my cheek. When he stirs, he remembers the outburst and is embarrassed, his big blue eyes and small voice plead for forgiveness, redemption and the knowledge that all is not lost. Again crossing the bridge of forgiveness, as pardon comes from Kevin and me, but my heart is broken by the realization that we are not much further along the ADD road than when we left thirty-two days ago. Part of me still clinging to the "and they lived happily ever after" that wasn't meant to be, at least in the way I predicted. Maybe, the big miracle through the miles did not come in the way I expected; instead, small miracles, my changed heart and shared memorable moments are the prize. Michael will take small steps of growth for now as we let go of high expectations and adjust to life without me as the conductor. We are being redefined as mother and son by the road of life, life with ADD, and that is OK, that in itself is a healthy lesson learned. This is how it will be, a few steps back then many more forward, to learn and grow, embracing life as his own. I believe with all my heart that Michael in the end, when responsible for himself and relieved of societal expectations will understand and accept the glorious gift he is and find peace and joy within. That hope is the only miracle I need.

West Virginia and Pennsylvania pass quickly. Kevin drives this final leg, fully engaged in the road warrior groove, knowing the release of driving long distance with ease. After the first two hundred miles, the rest are a breeze, really . . . the rhythm of the road takes over.

Kevin is a joy to travel with this last leg of our journey and on the road of life. We are powerful allies in this ADD battle. I fantasize about traveling together, with two backpacks in a convertible to road warrior once more. I love the adventure of the open highway, daily unknowns, and focusing without distraction on what is most important. Road warrior travel shows me creation, up close and personal. I breathe in the wide-open spaces and appreciate time with people who matter most in my life, unencumbered by the weight of things and the noise of routine.

Christine has been an intrepid traveler these last miles; she too, feels the pull of the West, cry of adventure and love of the outdoors. Her genetic lottery predisposed to my own. Will she travel west one day in search of herself, or life, or freedom she will think the road possesses? She is asking for her own fifty states goal, having embraced it as a meaningful pursuit.

Michael is again asleep, catching a rest when he can and tuning out the constant chatter of his sister. We see our first official "Welcome to Maryland" sign, and Christine squeals with delight, excited to be home and "not living out of the car." She chatters away, as she's earned her Native American name of "Chatty Squirrel," and it fits her to a tee! Our reentry celebration cheers do not stir Michael one bit. He is exhausted, anxious to be home, ready to be tucked in his own bed.

Lightening storms in the suddenly modest Maryland Mountains are treacherous and slow our progress. Significant rain and large hail are polka dotting the highway with multiple accidents. We stop for a safety break at eleven, seeking a reprieve from the pounding road conditions, and sit out the worst of the storms. Eating our fill of submarine sandwiches and strawberry ice cream, discussion ensues whether to stop for the night to avoid the storm tossed roadway. A unanimous family vote to push on, we are all too eager to sleep in our own beds tonight, so on we trek.

Searching for Delilah on the road occupies my mind. Hearing her radio show and voice is bittersweet because she will forever remind me of our journey's West, chasing the setting sun and covering a "few" more miles before our nine o'clock curfew struck. She was our companion along the way.

Punchy from the road, a guessing game for our estimated time of arrival begins. The object of the family game is to guess as close as possible without going over, the exact minute of arrival. Kevin, the driver, who usually has the most control over the game, guesses 12:30 a.m., Christine weighs in at 12:45 believing he is on to something, as I take 1:00a.m and Michael guesses 1:15. We watch the clock with bated breath to see who will win the mind numbing game so late at night. Michael wins, with a time of 1:15, as we pull down the driveway. We're home! With a group high-five we are elated to be home and cheer ourselves, our journey and each other. We made it!

Kevin finishes this day with 809 miles, driven by a single driver in a single day. Michael hustles to be the first Nolan to cross the finish line, straight through the front door, leaving us in his dust as Christine for the final time records our mileage in her log. I flee the Suburban for the comforts of home. Had I really lived out of the car for thirty three days and believed I was comfortable? My mind focused on running from a perceived confinement of home and daily life with disorders, believed this. Is it really over? What lessons will stay with me and what will be lost? I so yearn to know I make a difference!

Exhausted yet excited to drop into the comfort of our own beds. I go from room to room, seeing with fresh eyes, the family life we've created. I drink it in, cherishing my new vision and the eloquence of life's ability to speak. Genuine appreciation engulfs me, and I am grateful for my abundant life. I'm tucked in our cozy bed, enveloped in the security that comes with home. It is safe, known and I sleep peacefully, embraced by the hope of new beginnings.

EPILOGUE

I wake at noon, the first to stir, and don't know where I am. So many places these last thirty-four days, 9,659 miles traveled! I sit to a strong cup of black coffee that wakes me. Reminiscing over the travel terrain I am now ready to begin unpacking the Chief, an incredibly daunting task.

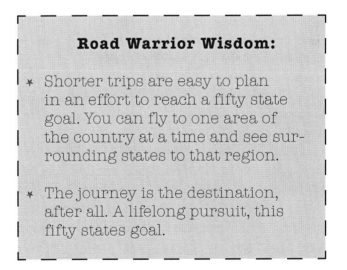

Road Warrior Wisdom:

* Shorter trips are easy to plan in an effort to reach a fifty state goal. You can fly to one area of the country at a time and see surrounding states to that region.

* The journey is the destination, after all. A lifelong pursuit, this fifty states goal.

I unload the car alone, by choice, needing to grieve the end of the journey. Every item removed has new meaning, having helped us survive the long journey West. Our only souvenirs are rocks, sugar cone pine cones and specialty foods, like buffalo jerky and Wisconsin cheese. I no longer want the weight of "things" to dominate my life, weigh me down, define me or hold center stage. Life, adventure and family are as conspicuous a consumption I now desire.

Westward ho and the spirit of adventure will always call to me, I no longer fight the feeling, I cannot! It is my nature, what speaks loudest and clearest to me. The soul searching, seeking and finding, that comes with long miles on the open road.

To see our great country, twice, in my old Suburban, is an experience I will always cherish. Sharing it first with Michael, and then again with Michael and Christine, that alone is a precious gift. I learned many things . . . about them, me, priorities and the true meaning of simplicity and family. I don't know when, or if, I will ever share such a special time alone with them again, in a car crossing the country. They grew up on our twenty-five states, two Canadian provinces adventure, me too! I am immensely proud of us.

I treasure the three weeks traveling with Kevin. I believe we could travel 'round the world and live to tell about it. Road warrior travel is a challenge, life lived on life's terms is not always easy but worth the lessons learned. We survived and thrived, both growing in significant ways, as individuals, and as a couple. He is my soul mate.

Ashley's arrival brought a breath of fresh air. She is positive and upbeat. She's a wonderful photo journalist and I am in awe of her eye, her ability to capture a moment. Her patience, kindness and fortitude gleam through with Michael, she's a great mentor. And, as importantly, she survived the wilderness! I believe Ashley heard and learned things about herself (and us) in the dense wilderness, but I am not sure she can hear it aloud in her soul, just yet.

The Curries are fellow Road Warriors who love this amazing country like we do. Tracy is organized and thoughtful, the perfect traveling companion, in tune with everyone's needs, generous with her love and patient and compassionate toward Michael. There is no one person I would rather travel the road of life with. Bruce and I are kindred, road warriors and adventurers to our very core. Never too tired for one more hike, a sunrise, evening stars, or campfire fun, he—like me—wants it all. We swear we will be National Park rangers when we grow up! His kindness and forbearance to Michael is a gift. The cousins, what a joy to be relatives and best friends! They have had so much fun together, have seen many spectacular sights and traveled the road of life, good and bad, as a clan. I earnestly pray they know how blessed this makes them.

As I settle into routine once again and daily life with special needs, it seems better this time, thanks to lessons learned on the road. I found I possess more courage and fortitude and love more deeply than I ever thought possible. I was not lost after all, but being redefined as a wife, a mother and a woman. With less haste in living life, reasonable expectations of myself, my family and others, and an appreciation for small sacred moments, cherishing simplicity and the newfound joy in ADD life. My family crossed the United States of America and back, together, TWICE! We saw each other in our finest moments like majestic snow capped mountain peaks and at our worst times in the depths of a dark deep valley. Changed, as forest fires raged and new growth appeared, this gestation revealing an authentic life. Growing like Sequoia trees, slowly, steadily, and with a strong, solid root that will survive the test of time and any elements the outside world presents.

I learned I cannot control the harsh judgments or high expectations of society toward my ADD/LD children. But, I now see clearly that true human nature and dignity are revealed in the way people treat a person with special needs and NOT the way the child struggling with imperfection tries to fit into the natural order of things. Do people grow from the experience of befriending a special need's child and learn that all special gifts are not packaged with a tidy bow? Do they learn through the child's pleading eyes, a humanity of inclusion, and what unconditional love looks like? This, the blessing and hope of ADD!

Christine is already on the telephone to her girlfriends reconnecting to her world. I hear "Chatty Squirrel" going a mile a minute catching up on news, with Missy, her kitten, snuggled on her lap purring. Christine rejoins them with a stronger sense of who she is and what she is capable of, having heard her own voice on the road loud and clear. Having her strong will and drama queen personality recognized and appreciated for the glorious gifts they are. Christine, knowing inside she can truly overcome any formidable odds and succeed. ADD no longer the central definition of Christine.

Michael, my big lovable Chesapeake Bay puppy! He is in the brackish brown creek jumping off the dock and splashing around freely. He, my true pioneer at heart! The creek, not even close to Crater Lake Blue, but home to the blue crab, great blue herons and us, and I am grateful for that. Michael is content to be home, surrounded by life on the Chesapeake Bay where he loves boating, skiing, crabbing and fishing. He knows unconditional love reigns and life with reasonable expectations dawns. He recognizes that there is a limitless, wide-open world out there just waiting for him, a world that fits him to a tee, when he's ready. He's dreaming of that world, and about his future, his dreams his own once again. He is smiling! I watch him from the window and feel proud of him. Proud to be Michael's Mom.

My Father's mantra from so long ago echoes in my ears, "Despite life's ups and downs, life is a joyous and wondrous adventure." Truer words I do not know. Trip West Two will soon be reduced to a carton of brochures, a photo album, scrapbook and brief video, taken by Michael "Spielberg" Nolan, his video journal of our Road Warrior adventure. None of this will ever truly contain how life changing a time this experience has been for me, for Michael and for our family. And finally, for our future with ADD! For now, Michael and I rest, as I plan and dream and hope until our next adventure calls. Westward Ho, the cry as old as the hills!

ONE YEAR LATER

I found my big miracle after all, and as lessons from the road have taught me in the past, it was where I least expected it, but maybe where I knew it was all along. The miracle for Michael and me is my changed heart. Fixing him I found was never the answer—fixing me was. Changing my attitude toward him and my expectations of him; no longer having to fit whatever mirage I set up as my mandate for his good life, the false confined life I expected him to live. Relinquishing my control and trusting God for a plan far greater than any of my own. Releasing my impatience and no longer hurrying his life along believing time and maturation would be the cure, instead causing me to miss the absolute joy of the journey, losing so many precious moments, time then forever lost.

Michael grew taller than me this past year, his voice strapping and deep, closing in on manhood and looking more like his father every day. A learner's permit set him free behind the wheel, and crew team chiseled his build. An independent trip to visit cousins in Las Vegas, he navigated the airport, ticketing and security as though a responsible old pro, negotiating the practical world on his own. Milestones of significant growth on his ADD journey; making him, strong, confident and capable.

His ADD, a precious gift and what makes Michael unique,

and now we find joy and humor in this life each day, even on bad days. The bad days are now few and far between, with long stretches of good days, happy days. The power of a changed heart should never be underestimated! Michael's life now lived with realistic expectations and goals he embraces as his own.

Michael and I watched with horror the devastation Hurricane Katrina wrought on New Orleans and the entire Gulf Coast region. Having traveled those highways and byways, met local folks (Gayle, among others) and walked the cobbled streets, we sadly saw a community and region we felt we knew personally, abruptly gone. The destruction appeared almost unfathomable and the human loss and suffering so profound. The fragility and fleeting state of life was once again so apparent.

Fifty states changed our life. Six years ago, when in utter exasperation Michael and I set out to see all fifty states, we had no idea where the road would lead. I only knew then that we were on the wrong road and that somehow the fifty states could change our path. And change our course it did. In ways that we would never have anticipated but that we are so grateful for.

A wide open world welcomed us, taught us life lessons we will never forget, and allowed Michael to see his great potential in a land he so loves. His world no longer confined and narrowed by starched blue blazer expectations. His life, his own, and with this change, his confidence in himself has grown exponentially, testing new waters formerly fraught with fear of failure are now opportunities, learning he can accomplish almost anything. Mistakes and missteps are no longer catastrophes, finding goals and dreams he now owns. Success, a reality! Michael knows a larger world than fifty states exists and is ready to conquer that world, wondering now if the seven continents is his next goal.

My life too changed in fifty states, finding a glorious release in embracing a new attitude toward our family life with ADD. Laughter, a regular part of our day now, at ourselves, at ADD related chaos and with each other. Michael's sense of humor is satirical and spirited, seeing life for what it really is, and cutting

Michael's Mom

through the niceties we have hidden behind in our effort to be excruciatingly polite never really saying what we truly mean. Yes, life is messy! And imperfect! And in messy, we have connected in a way I never imagined possible, truly engaging imperfection and being fully engaged with each other.

The road will always call to me and lucky for me I have another ADD child, Christine! I never imagined I would have believed that six years ago, lucky to have an ADD child. Christine wants her turn at fifty states, so back to the road we will go! Searching, seeking and finding our true selves, the selves we know we are created to be. ADD is a great blessing when I look at it through the right lens. My lens, the one formerly out of focus, is now clearly sharpened to see the joyous and wondrous adventure life with ADD is meant to be. I just had to get out of my own way to find the greener grass growing right under my own feet. Yes, messy is good.

· · · · · · · · · · · · · · · · · · · ·

I encourage you to write to me to share your own ADD success stories! Please send your letters to Terry Elizabeth Nolan at *Terry@michaelsmom.com* My next book is entitled, *Eating Paste; Childhood Adventures with ADD*. I will share your stories in this book with your written permission.

Tate Publishing & *Enterprises*

Tate Publishing is committed to excellence in the publishing industry. Our staff of highly trained professionals, including editors, graphic designers, and marketing personnel, work together to produce the very finest books available. The company reflects the philosophy established by the founders, based on Psalms 68:11,

"THE LORD GAVE THE WORD AND GREAT WAS THE COMPANY
OF THOSE WHO PUBLISHED IT."

If you would like further information, please call
1.888.361.9473
or visit our website
www.tatepublishing.com

Tate Publishing & *Enterprises*, LLC
127 E. Trade Center Terrace
Mustang, Oklahoma 73064 USA